Y Goeden Ioga

I Dad – dyn y pridd,
a ddysgodd i mi bwysigrwydd
y pethau bychain mewn bywyd.

Cyhoeddwyd gyntaf yn 2019 gan Wasg Gomer,
Llandysul, Ceredigion SA44 4JL
www.gomer.co.uk

Ail argraffiad – 2020

ISBN 978 978 1 78562 219 9

ⓗ testun: Leisa Mererid, 2019 ©
ⓗ lluniau: Cara Davies, 2019 ©

Mae Leisa Mererid a Cara Davies
wedi datgan eu hawl dan Ddeddf Hawlfreintiau,
Dyluniadau a Phatentau 1988 i gael eu cydnabod
fel awdur ac arlunydd y llyfr hwn.

Cedwir pob hawl. Ni chaniateir atgynhyrchu unrhyw ran
o'r cyhoeddiad hwn, na'i gadw mewn cyfundrefn
adferadwy, na'i drosglwyddo mewn unrhyw ddull na
thrwy unrhyw gyfrwng, electronig, electrostatig, tâp
magnetig, mecanyddol, ffotogopïo, recordio, nac fel arall,
heb ganiatâd ymlaen llaw gan y cyhoeddwyr.

Cyhoeddwyd gyda chymorth ariannol
Cyngor Llyfrau Cymru.

Argraffwyd a rhwymwyd yng Nghymru gan
Wasg Gomer, Llandysul, Ceredigion SA44 4JL

Y Goeden Ioga

Leisa Mererid

Darluniau gan Cara Davies

Gomer

Beth ydy ioga?

Ymarfer i'r corff, yr anadl a'r meddwl ydy ioga. Mae'r gair 'ioga' yn dod o'r iaith Sansgrit sy'n hen iaith o India, ac mae'n golygu 'uno' neu 'gysylltu'.

Mae'n ymarfer corff gwych am ei fod yn help i ymestyn a chryfhau ein cyhyrau, ond mae hefyd yn gallu ymestyn a chryfhau ein meddwl a'n hanadl.

Fel arfer rydyn ni'n anadlu i mewn ac allan drwy'r trwyn wrth wneud ioga. Mae'r anadlu dwfn yn helpu i dawelu ein meddyliau prysur ac yn gwneud i ni ymlacio a theimlo'n dda.

O ble daeth ioga?

Amser maith yn ôl yn India aeth pobl am dro i'r mynyddoedd a'r coedwigoedd i feddwl am fywyd. Roedden nhw'n eistedd gyda'u coesau wedi'u croesi yn edrych ar y byd o'u cwmpas. Dyma nhw'n dechrau sylwi ar fyd natur – y mynyddoedd mawr, y coed cryf a'r anifeiliaid ystwyth, a dechrau defnyddio eu cyrff i ddynwared beth roedden nhw'n ei weld, a dyma sut y dechreuodd siapiau ioga.

Mae ioga yn hen iawn, yn hŷn na'r coed sydd o'n cwmpas ni, hyd yn oed! Mae pobl wedi bod yn ymarfer ioga ers o leiaf 5,000 o flynyddoedd.

Croeso

Mae'r siapiau ioga yn y llyfr hwn wedi'u hysbrydoli gan fyd natur a chylch bywyd y goeden.

Wrth symud o un siâp i'r llall, fe fyddi di'n cael mynd ar daith gyda'r hedyn bach a bod yn rhan o'r stori.

Mae'n well ymarfer ioga yn droednoeth, ac mewn dillad llac, cyfforddus.

Mae'n syniad da i ymarfer ioga CYN i ti fwyta llond dy fol!

Gelli di ymarfer ar fat ioga neu ddod o hyd i le glân a diogel ar y llawr, neu beth am fynd allan i ganol byd natur?

Mae'n bwysig gwrando ar dy gorff a pheidio â gwthio, cystadlu na chymharu dy hun gydag eraill. Mae pawb yn wahanol ac yn unigryw!

Mae ioga yn addas i bawb – o bob oed, siâp a maint, felly defnyddia dy ddychymyg ac ymuna ar y daith!

Mae hedyn bach yn hedfan
yn uchel dros y ffridd;
mae'n dawnsio ar yr awel
cyn disgyn yn y pridd.

*Cofiwch wneud y symudiad hwn gyda'r ddwy fraich gyda'i gilydd.

Mae'r haul yn gwenu arno,
mae'n teimlo'n gynnes glyd.

Mae cwmwl yn dod heibio
a thywallt dafnau glaw;
mae'r hedyn bach yn deffro
gan symud troed a llaw.

Canghennau sy'n ymestyn o foncyff cadarn, cry', mae'r goeden nawr yn gartref, yn lloches ac yn dŷ.

mae'n adeiladu nyth bach

fel y gwnaeth sawl tro o'r blaen.

* Cofiwch wneud y symudiad hwn ar y goes dde a'r chwith yn eu tro.

Cyn hir bydd cywion bychain
yn trydar eisiau bwyd,
a mam yn chwilio'n brysur
am fwydyn blasus, llwyd.

Mae gwiwer fach yn sgrialu
cyn llenwi'i bochau mawr
â chnau a hadau bychain
a gasglodd ar y llawr.

Mae'r goeden yn llawn bywyd wrth dyfu tua'r haul,

* Cofiwch wneud y symudiad hwn i'r ddau gyfeiriad.

Daw eto hedyn arall
i hedfan dros y ffridd,

Dwi'n gorffwys fan hyn
yn llonydd a thawel.
Mae pob dim yn iawn,
dwi'n glyd ac yn ddiogel.

Mae hi'n amser i'r hedyn bach orffwys yn y pridd rŵan tan ddaw'r gwanwyn.

Beth am i ti aros yno wedi cyrlio'n gynnes, glyd fel yr hedyn bach a gorffwys ar y ddaear am dipyn bach?

Aaa! Dyna deimlad braf!

Mae'r symudiadau yn *Y Goeden Ioga* yn cysylltu sawl siâp ioga i greu dilyniant o symudiadau neu 'ddawns ioga'.

Rŵan rwyt ti'n barod am unrhyw beth!

Diolch

Diolch am ymarfer ioga gyda ni heddiw. Gobeithio dy fod wedi mwynhau.

Cofia fod yna lawer o siapiau ioga eraill i'w darganfod!

Mae'r symudiadau yn *Y Goeden Ioga* yn dilyn trefn gwers ioga arferol, yn dechrau gyda symudiadau i gynhesu'r corff, yna'n symud ymlaen i siapiau ioga sy'n cryfhau ac yn deffro'r corff a'r meddwl. Mae'n gorffen gyda siâp ioga sy'n ein helpu i ymlacio, i fod yn dawel ac yn llonydd.

Rydan ni'n anadlu ocsigen i mewn a charbon deuocsid allan.

Mae coed yn anadlu carbon deuocsid i mewn ac ocsigen allan.

Am bartneriaeth berffaith!

Wonderla

A NEW ALICE. A NEW MUSICAL.

Carly Rose Sonenclar (Chloe)

Photography by Paul Kolnik

Piano/Vocal Arrangements by John Nicholas

Cherry Lane Music Company
Director of Publications/Project Editor: Mark Phillips

ISBN 978-1-60378-372-9

Copyright © 2012 Cherry Lane Music Company
International Copyright Secured
All Rights Reserved

The music, text, design and graphics in this publication are protected by copyright law. Any duplication or transmission,
by any means, electronic, mechanical, photocopying, recording or otherwise, is an infringement of copyright.

Visit our website at www.cherrylaneprint.com

WONDERLAND

Wonderland is the giddy, soaring musical that plunges a new kind of Alice into a dazzling world of kaleidoscopic fantasy and romantic adventure. Returning to the strange universe of the classic "Alice in Wonderland," we find its timeless characters have evolved with the changing times but remain as familiar and endearing as ever. These residents of the Queen of Hearts' kingdom are now threatened by a new and madder Mad Hatter, whose dark ambition is matched only by her fearsome beauty.

Fantasy author Alice Cornwinkle is on the verge of a breakdown. Her life is a mess—she's distracted, overwhelmed and bewildered—and it's taking its toll. Her marriage to Jack is missing the romance it once had, her relationship with her daughter Chloe has lost its closeness, and her writing is suffering from a lack of imagination. In short, she is struggling with the same issues that plague most contemporary women.

Alice is berated by her publisher about "why the latest novel isn't finished yet." In addition to this humiliation, she's late for her Family Therapy session. Again. It's all falling apart! After the umpteenth disagreement with her soon-to-be-ex-husband Jack, she runs out of gas—figuratively, not literally—and falls asleep on her daughter's bed, surrounded by Chloe's "Alice in Wonderland" toys.

Her dream comes alive as a six-foot-tall White Rabbit entices Chloe away with him. Alice sees this just in the nick of time, and the chase is on. She is transported via a magical elevator into an astonishing Wonderland, where the issues of her life come up in encounters with a wild and eccentric bunch of extraordinary characters.

The analytical caterpillar has a taste for jazz and leggy chorus girls; El Gato is a grinning hipster cat in a '67 Impala. The White Rabbit is a messenger for the Queen of Hearts, and introduces Alice not only to an enchanted watch that can turn back time, but also to the White Knight, who bears an uncanny resemblance to her soon-to-be-ex, Jack.

All of the characters come together in a phantasmagoric garden at a Mad Tea Party, presided over by the villainous Mad Hatter, a woman with a very big secret, and the Queen of Hearts, a woman who is smarter than she first appears.

Although Alice tells everyone she meets in Wonderland that she's "looking for her lost child," it's not until the climax that she learns that the "lost child" she's looking for is not her daughter Chloe, but herself, and that what she needs is to see the world with the wonder and curiosity that she once had as a child.

With a memorably tuneful, enticing, moving score by Broadway's Frank Wildhorn *(Jekyll & Hyde)* and Jack Murphy *(The Civil War),* stunning dance from multiple Emmy award-winner and *Austin Powers* choreographer Marguerite Derricks, and as dazzling a scenic design as Broadway has seen, *Wonderland* is a deliriously funny, touching, life-affirming musical to stir the heart and delight the imagination.

Kate Shindle (The Mad Hatter)

Edward Staudenmayer (The White Rabbit)

CONTENTS

5	HOME
8	DOWN THE RABBIT HOLE
12	WELCOME TO WONDERLAND
24	DRINK ME
26	ADVICE FROM A CATERPILLAR
38	GO WITH THE FLOW
45	ONE KNIGHT
55	THE MAD HATTER
66	MAD TEA PARTY
70	HAIL THE QUEEN
75	A NICE LITTLE WALK
81	THROUGH THE LOOKING GLASS
89	I WILL PREVAIL
98	I AM MY OWN INVENTION
104	OFF WITH THEIR HEADS
111	ONCE MORE I CAN SEE
118	TOGETHER
129	HEROES
136	FINDING WONDERLAND

Karen Mason (The Queen of Hearts) and Ensemble

(left to right) Stefan Raulston, Julius Anthony Rubio, Darren Ritchie, Joey Calveri, Derek Ferguson

Janet Dacal (Alice) and E. Clayton Cornelius (Caterpillar)

Jose Llana (El Gato), Janet Dacal (Alice), and Ensemble

Home

Lyrics by
Jack Murphy

Music by
Frank Wildhorn

Chloe: Home is not a place, an ad-dress you mem-o-rize. It's more than sev-en flights or a-part-ment 8-A. It's where you nev-er feel lone-ly when—

F Fm C/G G7 Csus4 C
ev - er you're a - lone. That's how you know you are home.
G G/B Csus2
How I wish that we could feel that, some - how, right now.
B♭add2 Gsus4 G
How I wish that we could feel that a - gain.
C Em7 F F/G G
Home is like a smile you see in a pho - to - graph. No

matter what you do, it's not sup-posed to change. Why can't we all be to-geth-er the way we used to be? Back on the ground, no more rac-ing a-round. Here, safe and sound... And home.

Down the Rabbit Hole

Lyrics by
Jack Murphy

Music by
Frank Wildhorn

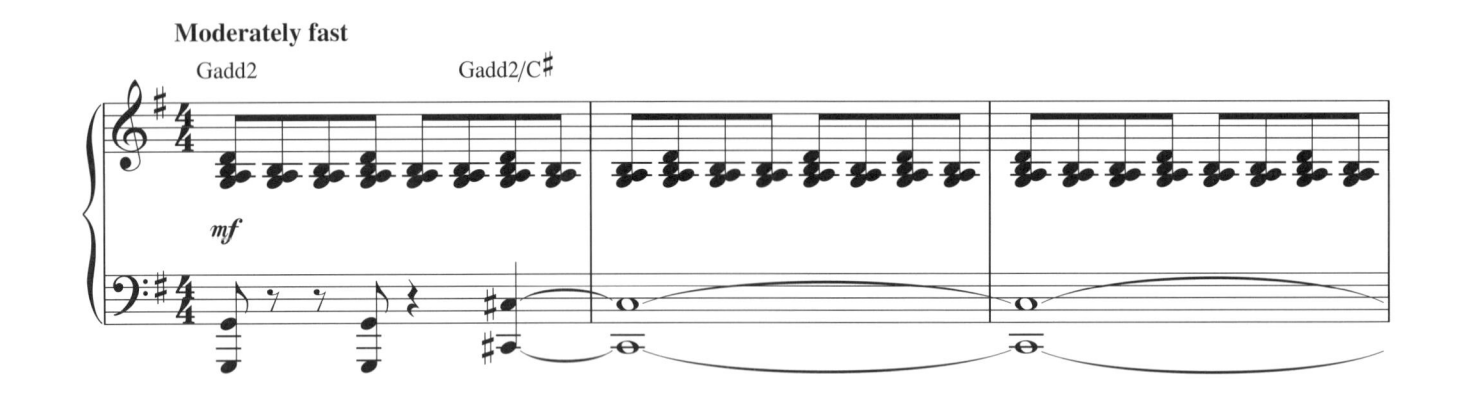

Moderately fast

Elevator voice: Down we go.   *Alice:* Oh, my God! Who are you?

Elevator: Just look out be - low! _____   *Alice:* Fear and doubt.

Copyright © 2011 Bronx Flash Music, Inc. (ASCAP), Ryan Samuel Melodies (ASCAP) and Lily Bird Music (BMI)
All Rights for the world Controlled and Administered by Bronx Flash Music, Inc. and Kenwon Music
International Copyright Secured   All Rights Reserved

Freak-ing out. Drop-ping way too fast!

Just re-lax! En-joy the view. *Relax.* *Alice:* You gotta be kidding me!

Elevator: Relax. *Alice:* How long will this last?

Down and down I go to God knows where!

Elevator: It's a spe-cial place with a lot of space and spe-cial peo-ple. *Alice:* Down I go, al-though when I get there, can you tell me when I'll get home a-gain? *Elevator:* Well, that's real-ly up to you...

Alice: What a fall... Could it be what I see is-n't real at all?

Welcome to Wonderland

Lyrics by
Jack Murphy

Music by
Frank Wildhorn

Moderately

Wonderland Voices:
Wel-come to Won-der-land. My God, it's half-past eight. Who cares if you came late.
We don't care where you've been. You're gon-na fit right in. A lit-tle fun de-tour.
A lit-tle cra-zy, sure. Don't get all in-se-cure.

Copyright © 2011 Bronx Flash Music, Inc. (ASCAP), Ryan Samuel Melodies (ASCAP) and Lily Bird Music (BMI)
All Rights for the world Controlled and Administered by Bronx Flash Music, Inc. and Kenwon Music
International Copyright Secured   All Rights Reserved

Pardon me, __ but have you seen someone looking like a queen __ sharp-ening __ a guil-lo-tine? __ Prob-'ly just as well.

She's ca-pri-cious as can be, lop-ping heads off by de-cree. __

This week sev-ered for-ty-three; cut-ting them pell-mell.
What a par-ty! Has it start-ed snow-ing? Ev-'ry-one not com-ing will be go-ing. Do you know the Queen of Hearts' new or-ders? They're the same as al-ways: close the bor-ders. Could she be the one, you know?

Bm/A
E7/G♯
G
D
Tin Man, Li - on, or Scare - crow? Wait, that's from a dif - f'rent show.
C
F♯+
Bm
Bm/A♯
Alice: Please start mak - ing sense. Wonderland Voices: Have you seen my wal - rus, dear?
Bm/A
E7/G♯
G
D
Big mous - tache that's down to here. Made the oys - ters dis - ap - pear,
C
F♯+
Bm
F♯
Bm
claim - ing self - de - fense. Wait, I think you
Alice: Wait, I think you think I think I'm

think you're dreaming.
dream - ing. And when I wake up, I'll wake up
You

wake up scream - ing. We don't think at all; we sim - ply
scream - ing.

feel, dear. Hey, la - dy,
Alice: O - K, some - one tell me what's the deal

here's the deal. Wel - come to Won - der - land.
here.

This is your new ad-dress. You'll love it more or __ less. No time to de-com-press.

It's af-ter-noon all __ day. There's lots of games to __ play.

Fla-min-go lawn cro-quet. So please en-joy your __ stay. __

Bm Bm/A♯ Bm/A E7/G♯
Ev - 'ry day, it's some - thing new. Prob - lems up the old wa - zoo.
G D C F♯+ Bm Bm/A♯
Ru - mors of a pal - ace coup. Alice: Get me out - ta here.
Wonderland Voices:
An - swers are in short sup - ply.
Bm/A E7/G♯ G D
Who, what, where, when, how, or why? Cross my heart and hope to die.
C F♯+ Bm C/B
Get it in - to gear. When your al - ter e - go's in - ter - fer - ing,

self - es - teem can - not help dis - ap - pear - ing.

Wel - come to Won - der - land. Start rock - in' with the band.

You're go - ing so damn fast. Your fu - ture's in your past.

An au - thor al - ways knows which way the sto - ry goes.

So tidy up loose ends with a little help from your friends. Come on and sing along and join our little band. Turn up the volume and keep on dancin'. Sit back, enjoy yourself, and feel the riv-er flow; ___ make sure the jour-ney's worth the

things you're chanc-in'. We're all a lit-tle nuts, in

case you did-n't know. ___ Oo - blee, ___ oo - blah. ___
Oo - blee, ___

oo - blah. ___ We'd love to stay ___ here ___ but we

really gotta go. Oo - blee, Oo - blee, oo - blah. oo - blah.

Life can be fan - tas - tic ev - 'ry min - ute for as long as you can just stay in it.

Wel - come to Won - der - land where ev - 'ry - thing you see,

Em
F♯7♯5
I mean from "A" to "Z," ain't what it seems to be.
Bm
G7
Wel - come to Won - der - land. Set phas - ers up to stun.
Em
F♯7♯5
Turn out the lights when done. Good luck and thanks a ton.
Bm
N.C.
Ciao, ba - by. Got - ta run.
3
3
Ped.
*

Drink Me

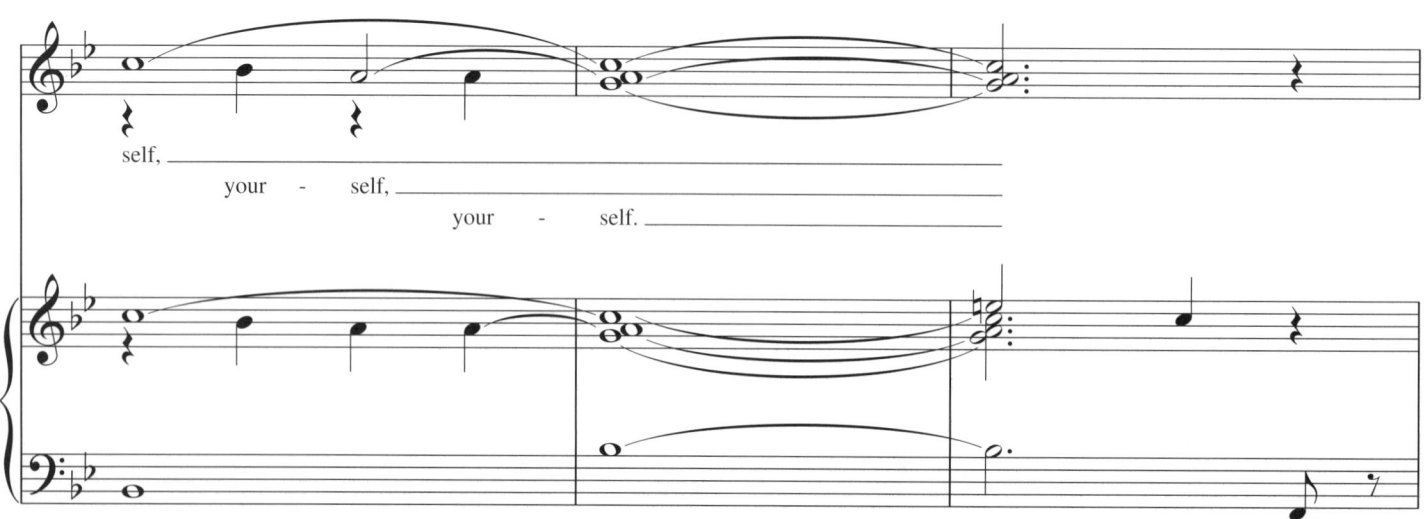

Lyrics by
Jack Murphy

Music by
Frank Wildhorn

Unearthly Voices: Bot-toms up. Take a drink, swim or sink till you find your- self, your- self, your- self.

It's a dream. If you blink, in a wink you'll a-wake. Run the risk.

A little slower

Take a chance. Cir-cum-stance will be good to you.

Make a door and then sim-ply walk right through…

Advice from a Caterpillar

Lyrics by
Jack Murphy

Music by
Frank Wildhorn

8-A as in "Alice." *Look, I can't seem to find the service elevator, but I'm hoping that whatever comes down must go up.* Caterpillar: Who are you?

Legs: Who are you? Who are you?

I - den - ti - ty is a trick - y, trick - y bus' - ness.

You think you're some - bod - y till sud - den - ly you're not.

You're not your name and you're not your ad - dress 'cause the

you who you re - mem - ber is who you for - got. Hey,

heed this ad - vice from a, a cat - er - pil - lar.

I know a thing or two of met-a-mor-pho-sis. Ow.

Fool's par-a-dise is you stand-ing still-er while the

riv-er rush-in' 'round you is the thing you miss.

Alice: The way you talk sounds like a for-tune cook-ie

in - stead of how things real - ly are. *Legs:* Tell us, who are

Caterpillar: Well, par - don me, let's take a look and see how the

you?

you that you been work - in' work - in' out so far.

So, tell us, who are

Dm7 Bb9 Em7b5 A7#5
Life is like jazz; things are al - ways chang - in'.
you? Ah, ah. Al - ways chang - in'.
Dm7 Bb9 Em7b5 A7#5
Just when you learn the tune, it's time to mod - u - late.
So tell us, who are
Dm7 Bb9 Em7b5 A7#5
Razz - a - ma - tazz riffs are re - ar - rang - in'. When the
you? Ah, ah. You bet - ter sing it in tune.

mel-o-dy is simple, then don't com-pli-cate.

So who are

Alice: It seems to me you on-ly speak in rid-dles you, you? Tell us true. So who are

and nev-er an-swer me at all, oh. you, you? Tell us true. Tell us, who are

Caterpillar: The more things change, the more they stay the same. From a you? True. dis-tance you look small-er, but you're just as tall. So who are So who are you? I'll re-peat, re-peat the ques-tion. So tell us who you

Dm7
B♭9
Em7♭5
A7♯5
Are you pre - pared to tell me what you're look - ing for?
are.
Tell us what you're look - ing
Dm7
B♭9
Em7♭5
A7♯5
You need a clue; well then, here's my sug - ges - tion: If you
for.
B♭9
Freely
A7♯5
can't see what's in front of you, then look some more.
rit.
Ooh.
Look some more.
rit.

Tempo I

Caterpillar: Hear what I'm sayin', girl. You think we brought you here so you can sit back and relax?

Legs: Be you ever so quick with vision keen:

By your eyes we are never seen,

unless, per-chance, it should come to pass you see our re-flec-tion in a look-ing glass.

Caterpillar: Tell you what-cha do:

Dm7 B♭9 Dm7 B♭9
Ev - 'ry time or two, while you're pass - in' through,
(Whispered:) Legs: Tell you what - cha do: Ev-'ry time or two,
Dm7 B♭9 Dm7 B♭9
from your point of view,
while you're pass - in' through, from your point of view…
Freely
Tacet
Dm(maj9)
find out "Who are you?"
Legs: …you?"
f

Go with the Flow

Lyrics by
Jack Murphy

Music by
Frank Wildhorn

Moderate Latin feel

El Gato: Bi-en-ve-ni-dos to the neigh-bor-hood hang. Say "bue-nos di-as" to the
You used to be the best mu-cha-cha there was be-fore you got so daz-zled

Copyright © 2011 Bronx Flash Music, Inc. (ASCAP), Ryan Samuel Melodies (ASCAP) and Lily Bird Music (BMI)
All Rights for the world Controlled and Administered by Bronx Flash Music, Inc. and Kenwon Music
International Copyright Secured   All Rights Reserved

rest of the gang. Pull up a stoop and let's relax for a while.
by all the buzz. The you you used to be you gotta go find,

El Gato's gonna 'splain the facts for a while. Life's un-pre-dict-a-ble. What
the part of you that some-how got left be-hind. Turn up the mu-sic and put

*Alice:
*1st verse only.

___ a news ___ flash! *El Gato:* I see you see how it is. ___ (O - ye co - mo
___ the top ___ down. Let the con-vert-i-ble cruise. ___ (Li - be - ra - te.) ___

va.) The best- laid plan of the mouse ___ and man ___ is to
Get some a - mi - gos and close ___ the shop ___ down and

Fmaj7/G
E7
E7♯5
im - pro - vise the things you plan to do. Get used to life on the brink,
lis - ten what El Ga - to says to you. My lit - tle Al - ice, be wise.
Am
Dm7
E7♯5
way out on a limb. You don't need to think when it is sink or swim.
You live on the ledge. Both: You don't an - a - lyze a - bout the cut - ting edge.
*Sing harmony 2nd time only.
Am
Dm7
D♯°7
No hes - i - tat - ing, no sense wait - ing. Why not
El Gato: Shut up and lis - ten to what's miss - in' till you
To Coda
Fmaj7/G
E
E7♯5
Am
E
jump right in and let the rhy - thm take you where you go with the flow.
hear the you you used to be and fi - nal - ly you go with the flow.

Am
E7
D.S. al Coda
E7♯5
Coda
Am
Dm7
E7♯5
You don't fight the tide and then let your in - tu - i - tion be your guide.
Am
Dm7
D♯°7
Get back your groove, then things im - prove when you have de -

cid - ed to stop fight-ing it and fi-nal-ly you go with the flow.

Don't need a les-son to stop your stress-in'.

Don't need a P-h.-D. (Es-cue-la en el bar-rio.) *For you to heal it,*

you got-ta feel it. Get it to-geth-er and then let it be.

"It's a guitar." Five, six, sev-en, eight!

Turn up the mu-sic and keep the top down. Let the con-vert-i-ble cruise.

Alice: Get in-to gear. Get some a-mi-gos and close the shop down and then

close your eyes and im-pro-vise a tran-quil-i-zer. Go with the flow. *Alice:* You go with the flow.

You go__ with the flow._____ You go__ with the flow.__
You gon - na go with the flow,_____ flow,_

with the __ flow. __

El Gato: You must learn to seize

op - por - tu - ni - ties. There's no un - der - tow go - ing with the flow._____

Oh,_ yeah!

One Knight

Lyrics by
Jack Murphy

Music by
Frank Wildhorn

Jack: Give me a dragon I can slay. Just say the word and I'll obey.
Show me a damsel in distress, and I'll save her.

Copyright © 2011 Bronx Flash Music, Inc. (ASCAP), Ryan Samuel Melodies (ASCAP) and Lily Bird Music (BMI)
All Rights for the world Controlled and Administered by Bronx Flash Music, Inc. and Kenwon Music
International Copyright Secured   All Rights Reserved

F♯
F♯maj7
If there's a mis - sion, I'm your man; throw in a la - dy if you can.
B6/F♯
Bm6/F♯
Though I am not Lan - ce - lot, I'll be brav - er.
Bsus2
F♯/A♯
Bsus2
I'll rush in to save the day. It - 'll look good on my ré -
F♯/A♯
Bsus2
A♯m7
su - mé. I don't care a - bout the take -
(Ré - su - mé.)

home pay; I just wan-na be, (I just wan-na be,

I wan-na be your one knight who'll fight
I wan-na be your one knight who'll fight.

and be your Won-der-land guide. One knight
Guide. One knight

in sight who has been board-cer-ti-fied.
in sight. Ah.)

C♯
Bsus2
F♯/C♯
You'll nev - er find an - oth - er one
C♯
A♯m7
like me. And e - ven if you ev - er do,
(If you ev -
Bm6
F♯
Bm6
show me one knight who will be half as
er do, show me one knight.)
F♯
B/D♯
Bm/D
F♯
true.
Now, listen here...
No mat - ter where you wan - na go,
mf

I'll take you there because you know the rules of chivalry aren't quite dead yet. So if you stick around with me, I promise you you're gonna see a happy ending riding into the sunset. When there is a real

__ close call, you need shin-ing ar-mor wall - to - wall and a knight __
(Wall - to - wall.)

__ like me __ 'cause, af - ter all, __ I just

wan - na be, I wan - na be your
(I just wan - na be, I wan - na be your

one knight, __ stage right, __ who nev - er miss - es his cue.
one knight, __ stage right. __ Cue.

One knight who'll smite
One knight who'll smite.
what-ev-er comes af-ter you. A knight who, when
You.
you ask, will al-ways say: Your ev-'ry wish is my com-mand.
It's my
I'm the one knight for Al-ice in Won-der-
com-mand. I'm the one knight for Al-ice in Won-der-

land. Please just give me half a chance. I'm an out-
land. Please just give me half a chance.

sourced knight so I work free-lance. I don't e-
I'm an out-sourced knight so I work free-lance.

ven need a real big advance. Just a
I don't need a real big advance.

kiss will do if I can be your
Just a kiss will do if I can be your

one knight; all right, tech-ni-c'lly two cred-its shy.
one knight. All right. Shy.

Still the one knight, bright white,
One knight, bright white.

but still a reg-u-lar guy. A knight who, when you ask, will al-
Guy.

ways say: Your ev-'ry wish is my com-mand.

A/E Dm6
I'm the one knight for this endeavor.
A/E Dm6 A/E Dm6
One knight, now and forever. The one knight for
A C♯m7/G♯
Alice in Wonderland.
f
mp
D/F♯ Dm/F Aadd2
Alice in Wonderland.

The Mad Hatter

Lyrics by
Jack Murphy

Music by
Frank Wildhorn

Hatter: Well, hello there, it's me with how it's gonna be. Settle down and listen up good.

Em
C7♯11
The old Hat - ter is gone but the hat must go on, worn by
Am7
me. Is that un - der - stood? So shut up and toe the line
B7
Em
Em/D
C7
while I re - de - fine how this all will be mine. I have a
Am7
B7sus4
B7♯5
dream that's got a full head of steam. What is

true, what is not, can both change in a shot, and, peo-ple, me, I could-n't care less

'cause in two sec-onds flat, liv-in' un-der my hat is the strat-e-gy for suc-cess. I will look the oth-er way when you wan-na play some-thing more than cro-quet. You catch my

Am7
B7sus4
B7
drift? My lit - tle per - son - al gift. I'm the
Em
C7
Mad Hat - ter. Come and fol - low me; this is it.
B7♯5
Em
The Mad Hat - ter. All
C7
B7♯5
Am
you got - ta do is sub - mit. And if you don't, my friend, well then,
f

in the end, there'll be noth-ing left to de-fend. Know what I mean?

When you are fac-in' the queen.

Up-per-

cased, dou-ble spaced, ev-'ry-one gets a taste and a brand-new leath-er hat-

band. But to par - tic - i - pate, let me re - it - er - ate, you must
(Give me the hat!)

first put me in com - mand. I'm the won - der, un - der - stand.

Un - der Won - der - land, put the reigns in my hands. I'll do the

rest as soon as you've ac - qui - esced.

B
Em
I'm the Mad Hat - ter, of -
(Mad Hat - ter, Mad Hat - ter.)
C7
B7♯5
Em
fer - in' a lit - tle bit more. The Mad
(So cra - zy. Mad Hat - ter,
C7
B
Hat - ter, giv - in' you what you're look - in' for. I am your
Mad Hat - ter.)
Am
B
Em
Em/D
best - worst case for the choice you face. I'm the fast - est rat in the race.

C7
Am
B7♯5
It's me or the queen
and her se - rene guil - lo -
Em(maj9)
F9
E9
tine.
There is
noth - ing
dim.
mp
E♭9
D9
D♭9
C9
I won't do.
There is
noth - ing
B9
Am7
too ta - boo.
I will lie.
I will
(She lies.
mf

cheat. I will track you down and then hit de-lete ____ tout'
(She cheats.)

suite. So, sweet-ie, ____ let me re-peat: ____

I'm the Mad Hatter, pledge
(Mad Hatter, Mad Hatter.)
allegiance while you still can. The Mad
(Uh, uh, uh. Mad Hatter,
Hatter, more than just a hat with a plan. I am where
Mad Hatter.)
you belong, the right kind of wrong, and I'll still be goin' real

strong. The bot-tom line is ev-'ry-thing will be fine as all the plan-ets a-lign. It's gon-na be so di-vine when all of this will be mine.

Mad Tea Party

Lyrics by
Jack Murphy

Music by
Frank Wildhorn

lo, good-bye. Let's see if pigs can real-ly fly. You know, the tea is all the way from In-di-a, you see. And though that is-n't near, it tastes as if we grew it here. Low tea, high tea, drink your own but don't drink my tea.

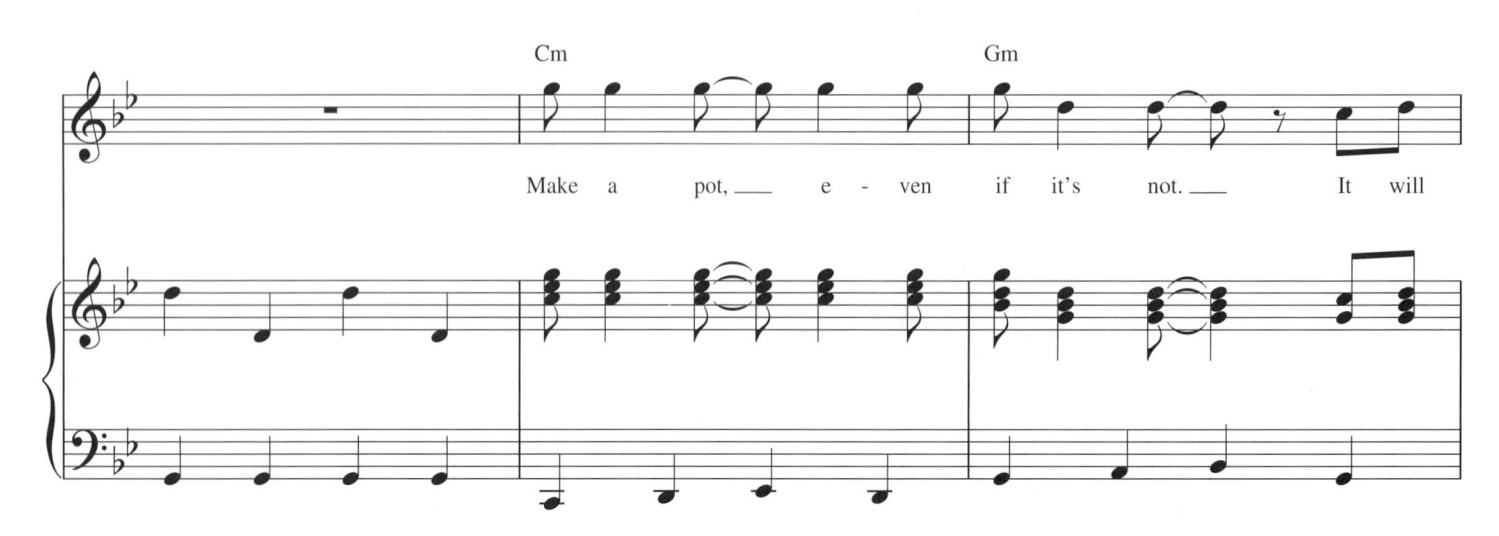

If there's tea, ___ well, then it must be ___ sum-mer-time in the late af-ter-noon.

Make a pot, ___ e-ven if it's not. ___ It will

To Coda

Ab7 ... **D7** **Gm** **N.C.**

be time for tea pret-ty soon.

Morris the March Hare: We're booked straight up through the apocalypse.

The name of the reservation?   *Alice:* Alice.   *Morris:* Goodie.

D7b5

Ensemble: Low tea, high tea, drink your own but

D.S. al Coda

don't drink my tea.

Coda

Hail the Queen

Lyrics by
Jack Murphy

Music by
Frank Wildhorn

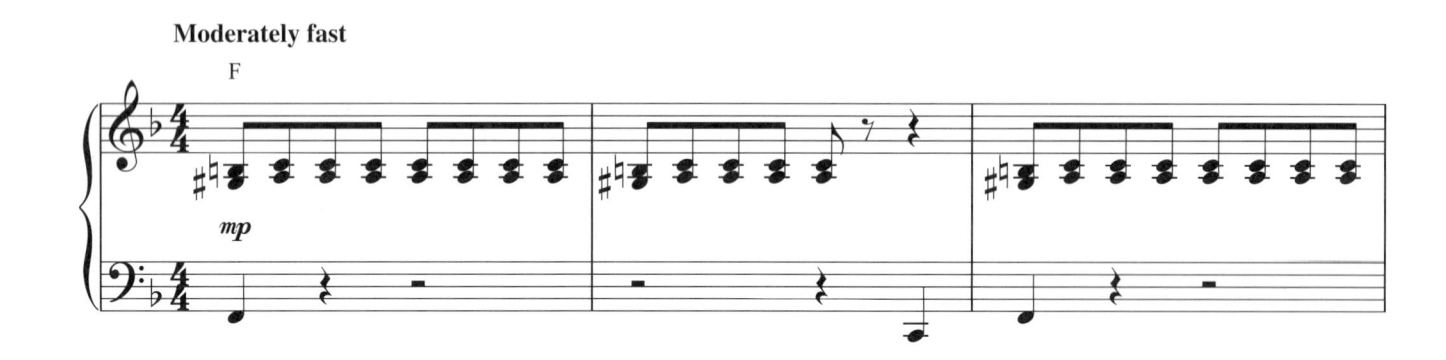

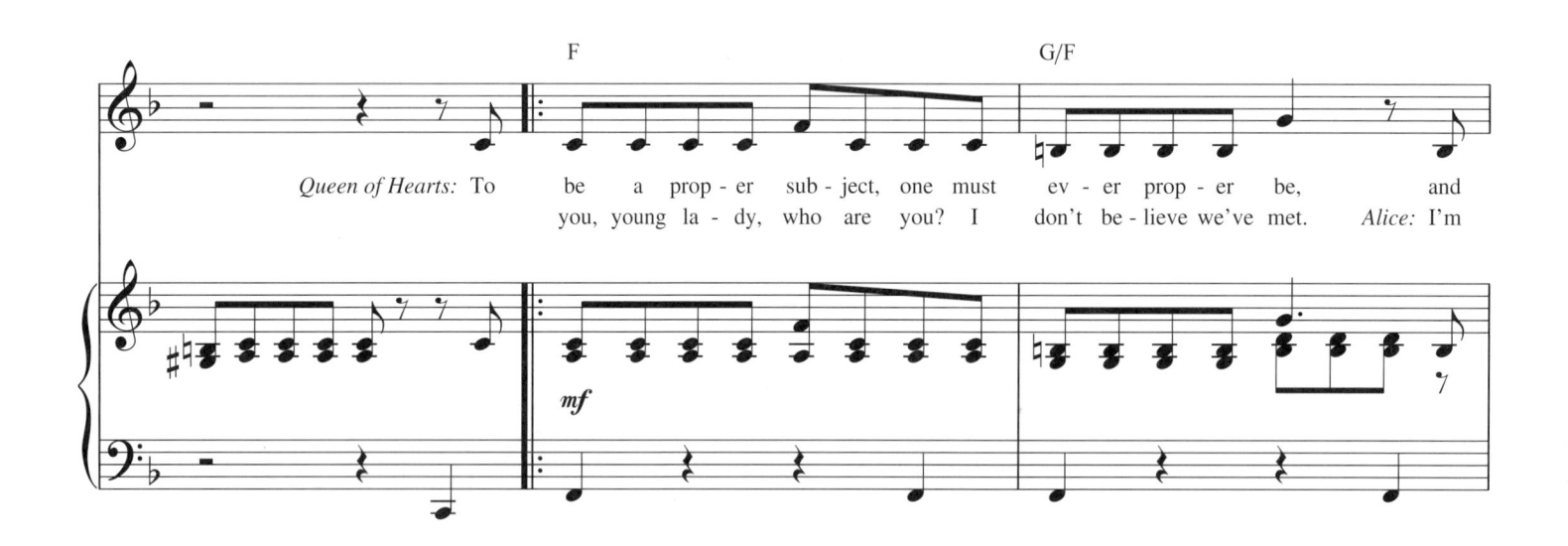

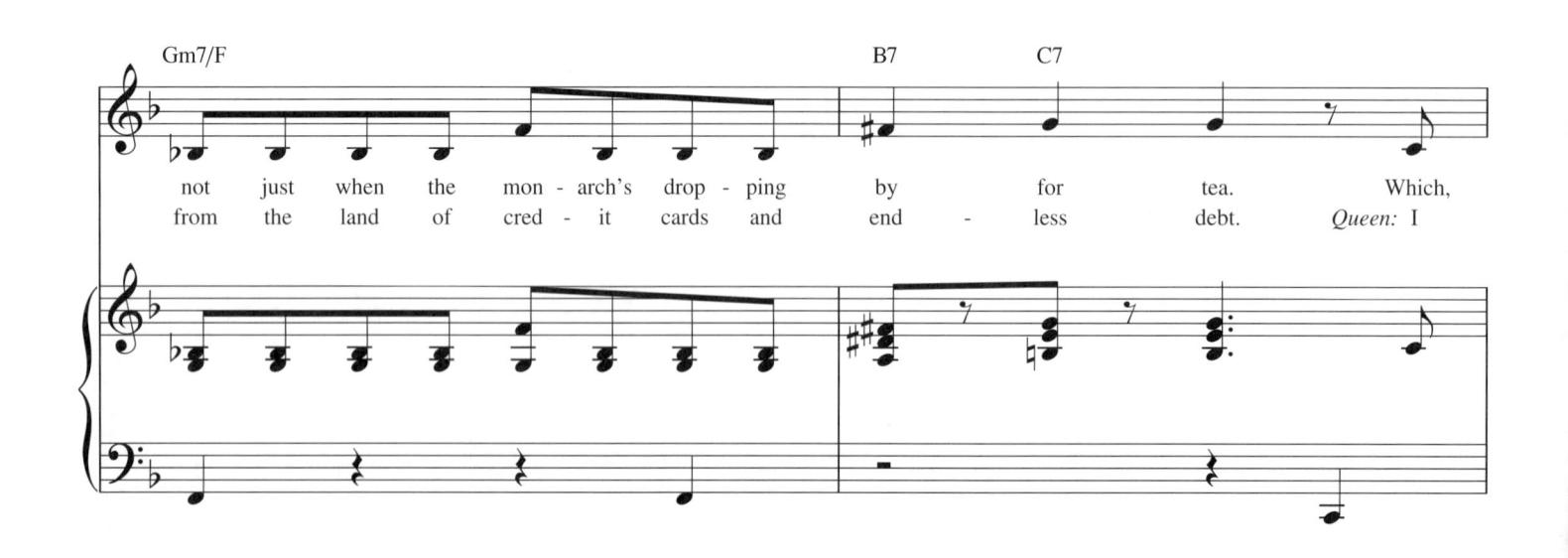

Moderately fast

Queen of Hearts: To be a prop-er sub-ject, one must ev-er prop-er be, and not just when the mon-arch's drop-ping by for tea. Which,

you, young la-dy, who are you? I don't be-lieve we've met. Alice: I'm from the land of cred-it cards and end-less debt. *Queen:* I

Copyright © 2011 Bronx Flash Music, Inc. (ASCAP), Ryan Samuel Melodies (ASCAP) and Lily Bird Music (BMI)
All Rights for the world Controlled and Administered by Bronx Flash Music, Inc. and Kenwon Music
International Copyright Secured   All Rights Reserved

[F] by the way, reminds me: Was my [G/F] invitation lost? *Rabbit:* Per-
see; that sounds an awful place. No wonder you've come here. No

[Gm7/F] haps the palace mailroom got their signals crossed. [B7] Well, in [C7] *Queen:*
matter here or there, let me make one thing clear: If you

[F] either case, they [C/E] face dis- [Dm7] grace, so [F/C] let's be- gin the [B♭] ex- e-
an- ger me, there'll be no tea and very little sym- pa-

[C°7] cu- [C7] tion. *Crowd:* Yes, in [F] either case, they [C/E] face dis- [Dm7] grace. All [F/C]
thiz- ing. *Crowd:* There will be no tea, says Her Maj- es- ty. All

1. hail the queen. *Queen:* And

2. queen. *Jack:* Your maj-es-ty is right, of course. *Queen:* Of course I am; I am the source, and will not suf-fer those who dis-a-gree. *Jack:* Like Twee-dle-dum and Twee-dle-dee, she will heart-ed-ly a-gree, Your High-ness. *Alice:* I do a-gree, Your Maj-es-ty. If I a-gree, is there a fee? There will be if you sing the song off-key.

Jack: We crave a boon from you, my queen, more of a roy-al fa-vor. *Queen:* Wheth-er large or small or none at all, you must be care-ful what you wish for. Wheth-er large or small or none at all, all

hail the queen.

A Nice Little Walk

Lyrics by
Jack Murphy

Music by
Frank Wildhorn

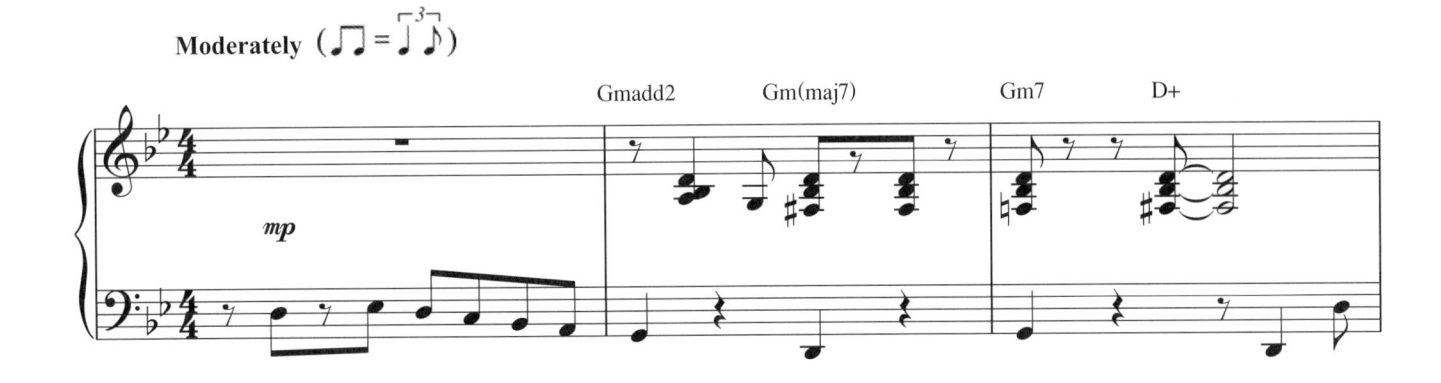

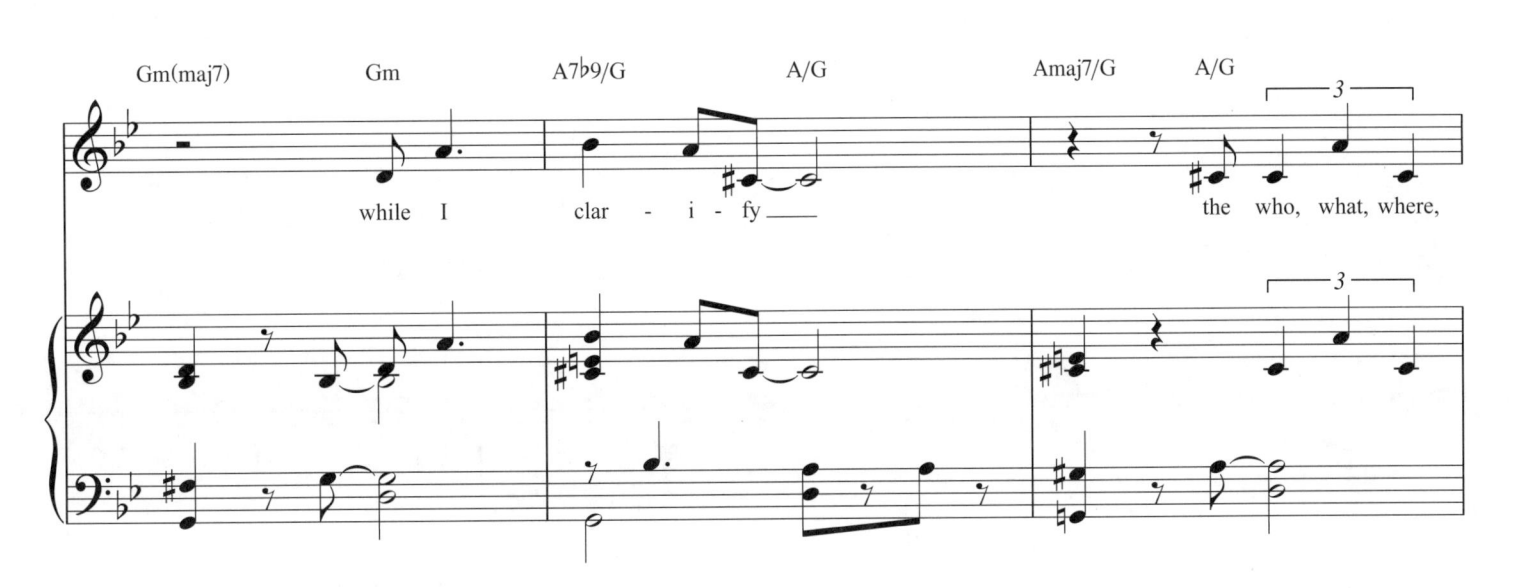

Hatter: A nice little walk while I clarify the who, what, where,

Copyright © 2011 Bronx Flash Music, Inc. (ASCAP), Ryan Samuel Melodies (ASCAP) and Lily Bird Music (BMI)
All Rights for the world Controlled and Administered by Bronx Flash Music, Inc. and Kenwon Music
International Copyright Secured   All Rights Reserved

Cm7 Cm6 A♭/C Cm6 D7♭9
when, and why — of Mom's pe - cu - liar con - nec - tion to
Dad's im - per - fec - tion. Morris: A nice lit - tle walk. —
Gmadd2 Gm Gm(maj7) Gm
Hatter: Par - tic - i -
A7♭9 A Amaj7 A Cm7 Cm6
pate with me Both: in fam - 'ly ther - a - py
D7 Gm6 G7♭9 G7 D♭9♯5
Hatter: till we're all guilt - free. Be of good

Cm9
A7♭9
N.C.
cheer, Morris: dear. Hatter: Noth - ing's as bad as at first it seems,
mf
D♭9♯5
Cm9
A7♭9
once we're an - a - lyz - ing your
Morris: A
Cm6/D
D7♭9♯5
Gmadd2
Gm
dreams.
A nice lit - tle walk
theme park of Freud - i - an themes.
A nice lit - tle walk.
f
mp
Gm(maj7)
Gm
A7♭9
A
Amaj7
A
might help us un - der - stand
till hand in
Un - der - stand.

Cm7
Cm6
D7♭9
Gmadd2
Gm(maj7)
E♭7
hand, Morris: in hand,
Hatter: Mom and you,
Gmadd2
Gm(maj7)
E♭7
D7♭9♯5
Gmadd2
Gm(maj7)
Morris: and Dad, too,
Both: all break through.
Gm7
D+
Gmadd2
Gm(maj7)
Gm7
D+
Cm
Cm6
E♭/A
Cm/E♭
A♭/E♭
D7
mf cresc.

G7♭9
Cm9
A7♭9
Take it from me.
See, *Hatter:* man - ag - ing stress is our
N.C.
Cm7
Cm7/B♭
spe - cial - ty.
Hatter: Warm tea…
Morris: Warm tea
A13♭9
E♭°7
D7♯5
Trust - ing in me is the key.
A
and some trust is the key.
8va
mp
Gmadd2
Gm
Gm(maj7)
Gm
A7♭9
A
nice lit - tle walk
Morris scats…
Hatter: or we can ride in - stead.
Morris scats…

Amaj7 A Cm7 Cm6 D7
Hatter: All a - board my new sled
Morris: to her hive. _
Gmadd2 Gm(maj7) E♭7 Gmadd2 Gm(maj7)
Freely
E♭7 Tacet
Hatter: Big high - five.
Both: You can
Tempo I
Gmadd2 Gm(maj7) Gm7 D+ Gmadd2 Gm(maj7)
drive.
mf
Gm7 D+ Gmadd2 Gm(maj7) Gm7 D7♯5 Gm

Through the Looking Glass

Lyrics by
Jack Murphy

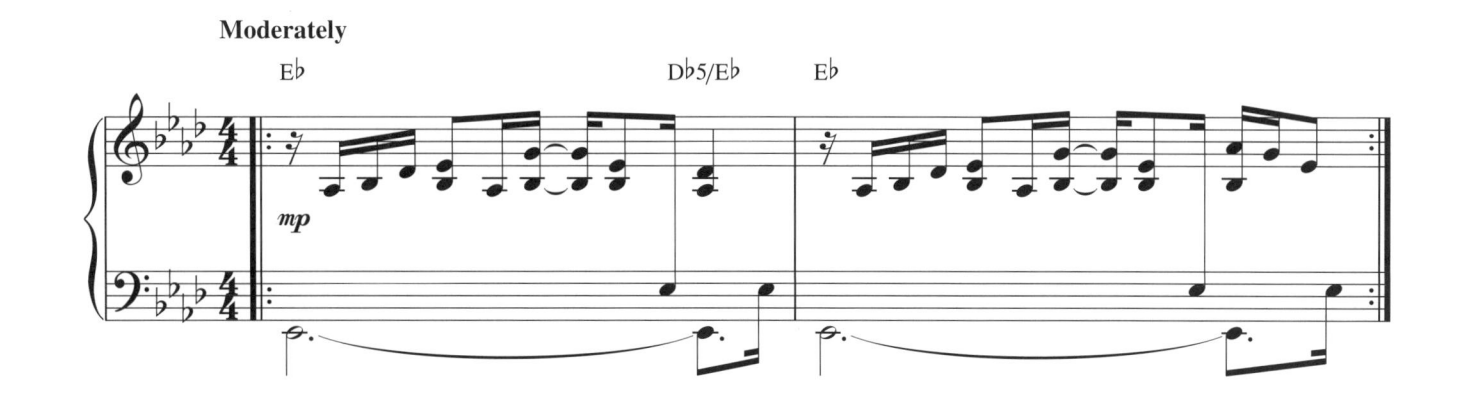

Music by
Frank Wildhorn

Jack: Through the looking glass we go, risking ev-'ry-thing for what might be, all the things_ you used_ to know_ when your heart_ was young_ e-nough to_ see,_ *El Gato:* through your_ own_ re-flec-tion, *Caterpillar:* past your_ im-per-fec-tion. *Rabbit:* It's so in-tim-i-dat-ing. *Jack, El Gato, Rabbit, Caterpillar:* No more_ hes-i-tat-ing. *Jack:* Through the look-ing glass_ we go,_

where the world is in reverse and the ending always starts a new beginning.

Jack, El Gato, Rabbit, Caterpillar: Through the mirror, even though things might go from bad to worse, *Jack:* close your eyes, let go and learn to believe so we can pass *Jack, El Gato, Rabbit, Caterpillar:* through the looking glass.

El Gato, Caterpillar: Here we come, so clear the deck. Bombs a-way and then look out be-low.

Alice: Bombs a-way, look out be-low. *Rabbit:* I am such a nerv-ous wreck. Don't know up from down or friend from foe.

Jack: Fear will make you braver, brave enough to save her.

Alice: All of you and me then... *All:* Get set: One, two, three, and...

Through the looking glass we go, where the front is always back

and what's left is right and sometimes wrong is righter.

Through the mirror, even though night is day and white is black,

Alice: as my crazy life begins to approach critical mass...

Jack, El Gato, Rabbit, Caterpillar: Through the looking glass. Strange but true, something's changing deep inside me, breaking through,

waking what's asleep inside me. All at once,
I know where it is I'm going to, and what to do.

Jack, El Gato, Rabbit, Caterpillar: Through the looking glass we go towards the opposite of me, where clock tower's hours Yeah.

Company: Through the looking glass we go, all run counter-clockwise, through the nightmares in our way. Through the mirror we all go...

Alice: Through the looking glass!

I Will Prevail

Lyrics by
Jack Murphy

Music by
Frank Wildhorn

Hatter: A child believes the best in you. And that belief

al - ways makes the dark - est lies seem al - most true. A sleight of hand, this "al - most truth," can be - guile the pur - est youth to Won - der -

land.

Now ev-'ry piece is in place, and all that's left to e-rase be-fore I take o-ver all the pow-er is ev-'ry trace of dear Al-ice, then the queen.

She's been a thorn in my side ___ and she can run but can't hide. ___ We're fast approaching the witching hour, and settling scores ___ is my routine. ___ Oh, well. All's ___ well, ends ___ well.

A/E E A/E Esus4 G D G
Fare - well, Al - ice. Too late. Check -
D G C♯sus4 C♯
Half-time feel
(♩ = 𝅗𝅥) F♯m
mate is your fate. It's o - ver. I come
I will
rit. e cresc.
f
a tempo
D E E/G♯ A E/G♯ F♯m
a - live when you're a - fraid. I'll write the
sur - vive and you will fade, a with - ered
1.
D Esus4 E C♯
ending of your trag - ic fair - y tale.
flow - er, small and

frail, ____ while I pre - vail. ____

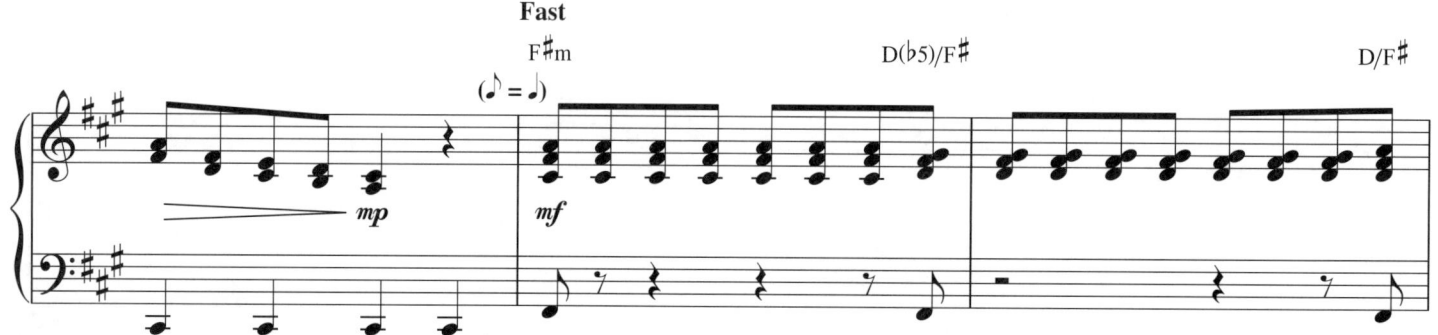

This time it's gonna be me.

The last thing you'll ev-er see, an ar-ma-ged-don of my de-vis-ing.

There's no way you can es-cape from what I do.

So leave your half-heart-ed souls for me to bul-ly and rule.

The sly magician of compromising, to conjure all that is false until it's true.

Poor Jack, blackjack, sad sack, fallen hero.

Bad news, you lose. Light the fuse. It's over.

rit. e cresc.

Half-time feel
Am F G G/B C G/B
You die, I thrive; and so it goes.
I will sur - vive, and heav - en knows,
f
a tempo
Am F Gsus4 G
1.
I am the ending of your trag - ic fair - y
there is no way that I can
E
tale.
2.
Esus4
fail.
Freely
E Tacet
Fast
Amsus2 Fmaj7/G
I will pre - vail.
rit.
Fmaj13 Dm6/9 Am

I Am My Own Invention

Lyrics by
Jack Murphy

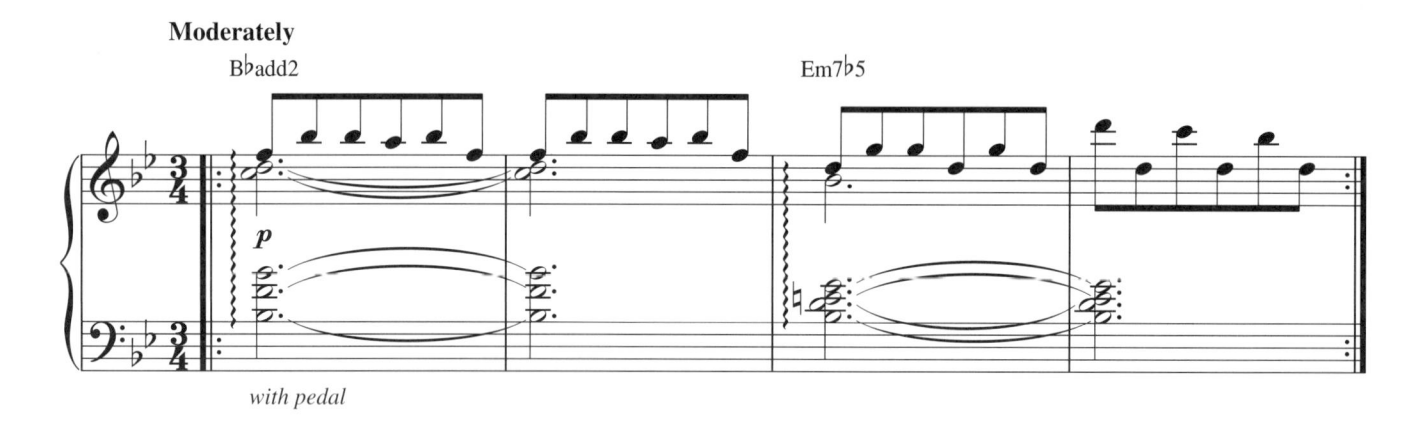

Music by
Frank Wildhorn

The Victorian Gentleman:

Noth-ing can ex-ist till you dream it first; ev-'ry-one knows this.
Not the way things are, but how they should be; this is what is true.

Then it will ar-rive, new and un-re-hearsed, viv-id as a kiss.
Wish up-on a star, close your eyes and see all that you can do.

*Dreamers and children can conjure things easily,
things their eyes, though they're closed, can see.*

Try to remember the way you were when you were her, the little girl that's there inside of you.

I am my own in-

ven - tion, meet-ing each day ____ a-

new. _____ Can you i - mag - ine

be - ing _____ your own in - ven - tion

too?

with pedal

B♭add2
Em7♭5/B♭
Dreams will al - ways start with a hap - py end wait - ing to come true.
mp
B♭add2
Lu - cid as a heart, wel - come as a friend,
Alice: So long a - go.
Em7♭5/B♭
E♭maj7
gos - sa - mer and new.
Help me so I can re -
B♭add2/D
Cm7add4
mem - ber dreams to share with dreams to spare, i - mag - in - ing a

F7sus4
Cm7/F
dream - er just like you.
B
F♯/G♯
C♯m7
F♯sus4
F♯
Both: I am my own in - ven - tion.
mf
B
F♯/G♯
F♯m7
A/B
Fi - nal - ly I can see.
E
B/D♯
The Victorian Gentleman:
I am my own in - ven - tion.
Alice: I am my

C♯m7
Badd2/D♯
C♯m7
To - mor - row can't be
Both: all it should
own in - ven - tion.
Badd2/D♯
C♯m7
G/A
Gmaj7/A
be till I've in - vent - ed
C♯m7/F♯
F♯
B
me.
f
Emaj7
E
B
rit.

Off with Their Heads

Lyrics by
Jack Murphy

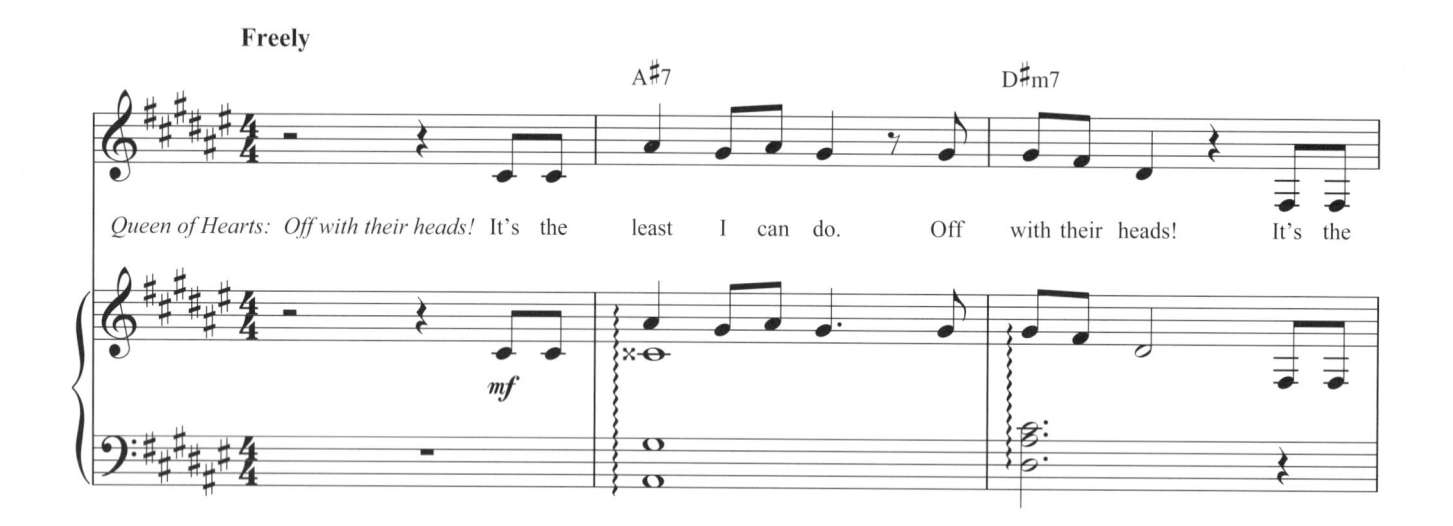

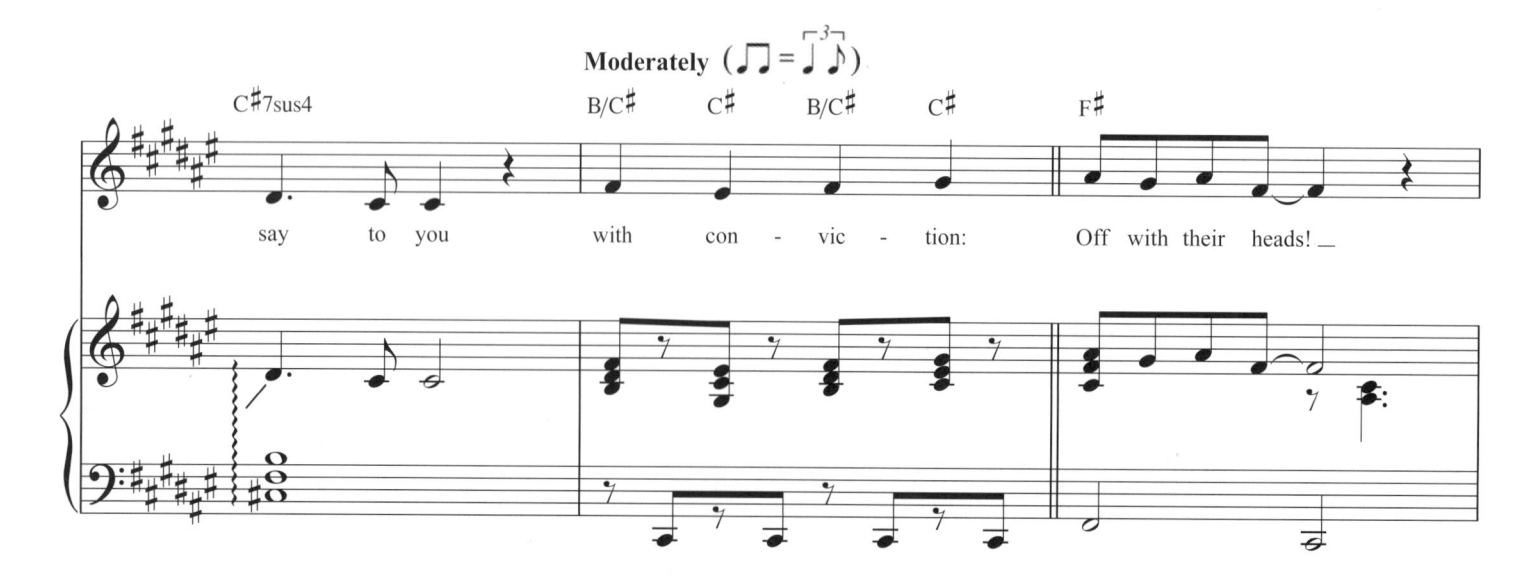

Music by
Frank Wildhorn

Freely

Queen of Hearts: Off with their heads! It's the least I can do. Off with their heads! It's the only phrase that always rings true. Never gets old. So I say to you with conviction: Off with their heads!

It's my one real mi-lieu. Ev-'ry-one dreads what the queen may say. Though hats they may doff, it will be off with their heads.

Ooh! I try to be e-ven and fair, but as you see, I'm al-most nev-er all quite there. No-blesse o-blige,

Ladies-in-Waiting: She tries to be e-ven and fair, but as we see...

Freely
F7/A
B/C♯
C♯
Bmaj7/C♯
C♯7♭9
my der - ri - ère.
Ladies: Her der - ri - ère.
rit.
Moderately
F♯
Sweet. When I de - mand, all must ad - here.
Ladies: It's real - ly grand,
F7
F♯
I wave my hand and all my
the roy - al rear. Can she com - mand?
D♯7
G♯m7
F7/A
cour - ti - ers ap - pear. And when they don't, or

if they won't, loud and clear, it's "Off with their heads!" I don't care what they've done. "Off with their heads!" is my first and sec-ond rule

Ladies: This is her...

num-ber one. Once you've be-gun, well, it's so much fun. All to-geth-er... "Off with their heads!" is a man-tra of mine.

"Off with their heads!" is my bottom line. And if you dare scoff,
Ladies: Fine.

well, then it's off with your head!
Ladies: She's off, she's awful, she's all

off with your heads!

Don't need a congress or a constitution, for it's a foregone conclusion

that ev-'ry prob-lem has the same so-lu-tion. Per-suade, cru-sade with a cus-tom-made re-new-a-ble, do-a-ble, un-mis-con-stru-a-ble stain-less steel blade. Off with their heads! It's the least I can do. "Off with their heads!" is the on-ly phrase that al - ways rings true. Ba - by, it's off, off, off, off, off, off, off, off, off, off with their heads. Off with their heads. Off with their heads.

(Whispered:)
Mama says off with their heads. Yeah!

Once More I Can See

Lyrics by
Jack Murphy

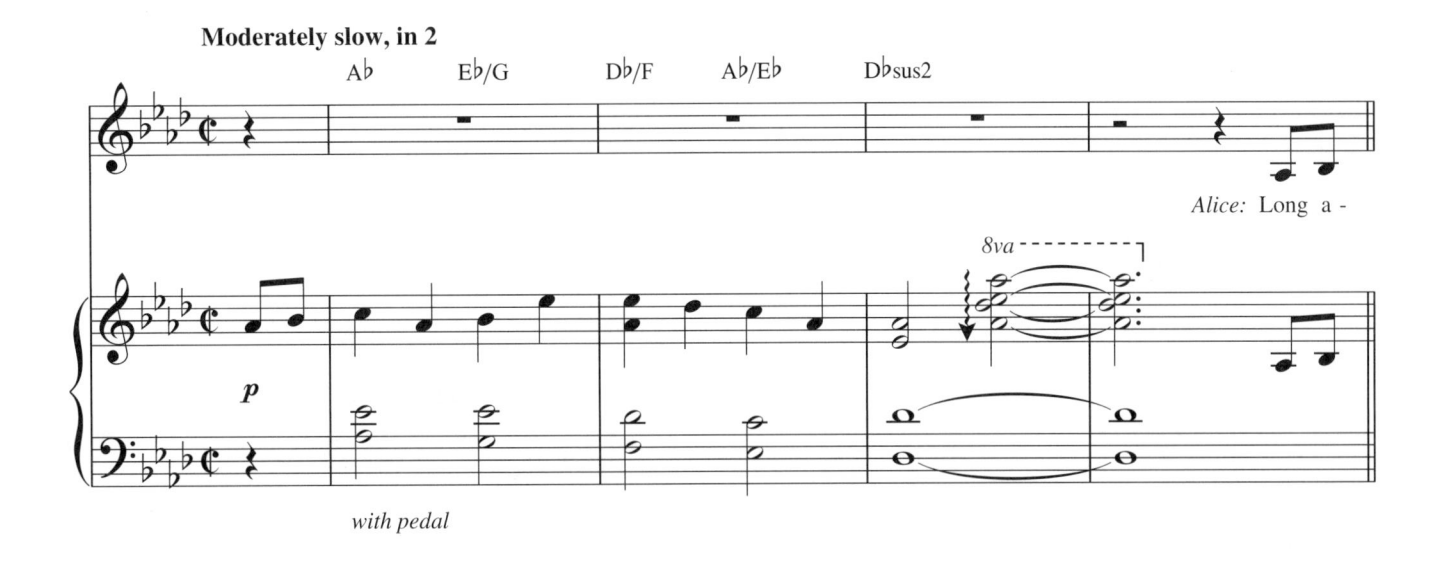

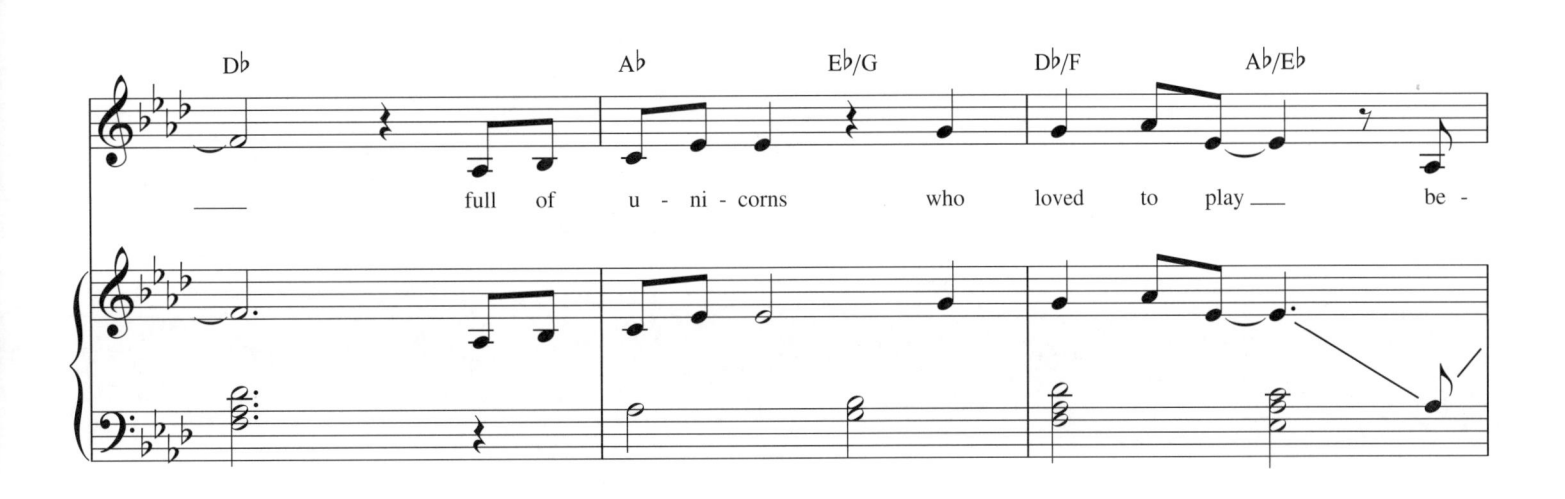

Music by
Frank Wildhorn

Alice: Long ago and, oh, so far away, there were dreams that I recall, full of unicorns who loved to play be-

Copyright © 2011 Bronx Flash Music, Inc. (ASCAP), Ryan Samuel Melodies (ASCAP) and Lily Bird Music (BMI)
All Rights for the world Controlled and Administered by Bronx Flash Music, Inc. and Kenwon Music
International Copyright Secured   All Rights Reserved

hind my gar-den wall. And the clouds would look like drag--on's tails as they moved a-cross the sky. And a tree could be the Prince of Wales, and lit-tle girls could fly. I re-mem-ber ev-'ry mo-ment, how it was to just be me. And to my sur-prise, I look through your eyes, and once more I can see.

I re-member living in be-tween what was real and what is not, 'neath a sky of blue and field of green I long ago forgot. And I remember rabbits running late underneath my mother's fence, and a singing cup and talking plate who somehow both made sense.

Ebsus4 Eb Ab Eb/G Db
I re - mem - ber ev - 'ry mo - ment. I re -
Ab Eb/G Db
mem - ber be - ing free. And to
Ab Eb/G Db/F Ab/Eb
my sur - prise, I look through your eyes and
Bbm7 Db/Eb Absus4 Ab
I re - mem - ber me. For

somewhere deep inside me, there's a girl from way back when. She just needs your heart to guide me and make her see again. I remember ev'ry moment when my

A E/A D E A E/G♯
heart was young and free. And to my sur - prise, I
D/F♯ A/E
3
look through your eyes and
mp
Bm7 D/E Tacet A E/G♯
once more I can see.
rit.
a tempo
p
D/F♯ A/E Dsus2 A
rit.

Together

Lyrics by
Jack Murphy

Music by
Frank Wildhorn

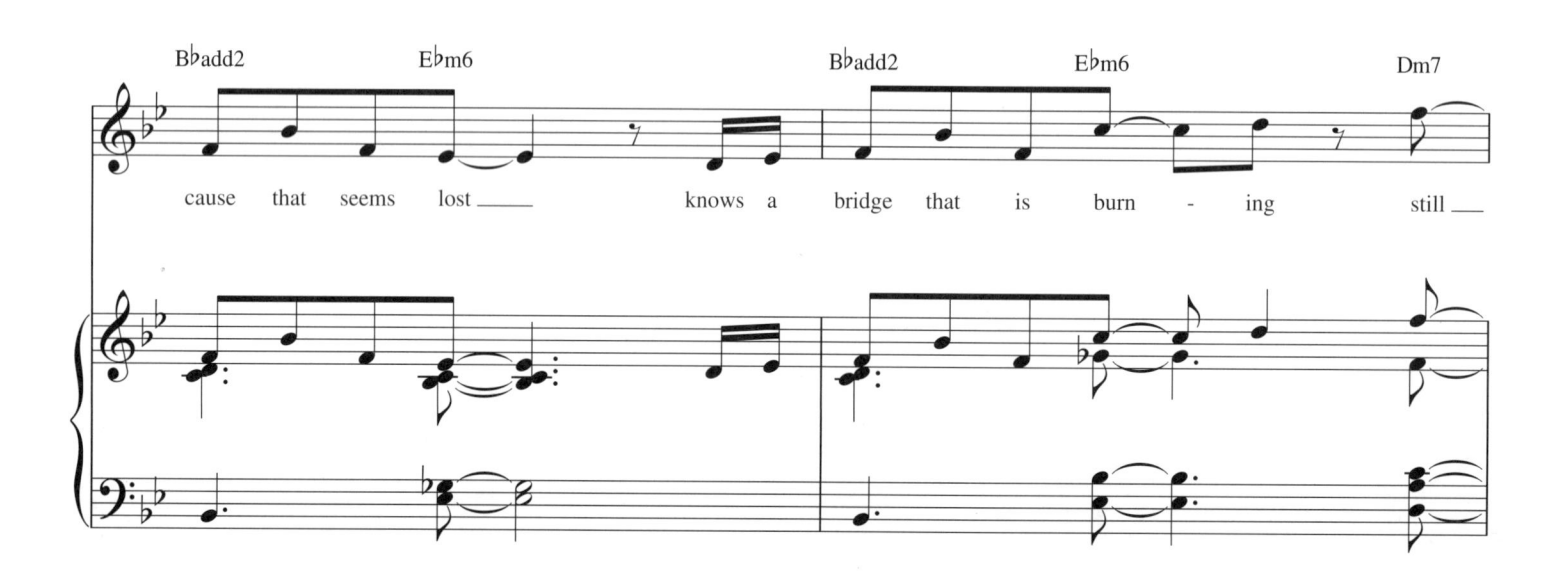

Moderately, freely

Jack: Ev - 'ry knight who is yearn - ing for a cause that seems lost ___ knows a bridge that is burn - ing still ___

Copyright © 2011 Bronx Flash Music, Inc. (ASCAP), Ryan Samuel Melodies (ASCAP) and Lily Bird Music (BMI)
All Rights for the world Controlled and Administered by Bronx Flash Music, Inc. and Kenwon Music
International Copyright Secured   All Rights Reserved

Gm7
Cm7
can be crossed.
Got - ta keep on be - liev - ing 'cause be -
Slightly faster, with a steady beat
Cm7/F
B♭sus2
G♭maj7/A♭
E♭/F
liev - ing can make it true.
Caterpillar, El Gato:
You've got to just be - lieve in you.
Jack: There's a
mf
B♭
E♭m6
he - ro in - side you
who's been there all a - long,
stand - ing
Dm7
right there be - side you,
sing - ing your song
with a
Caterpillar, El Gato: Sing - ing your song.

sense of di - rec - tion and a whole new con - nec - tion.

Jack, Caterpillar, El Gato:
We're gon - na make it, my friend. *Jack:* To - geth - er we're

gon - na make it through the dark - est night. *Jack:* To - geth - er we're
Caterpillar, El Gato:
To - geth - er.

gon - na make it. *El Gato:* Gon - na make it back home. *Jack:* To - geth - er we're
To - geth - er.

gon - na ___ make ___ it. Gon - na stand up and fight _____ 'cause be -
To - geth - er. ___

fore this is o - ver, *Jack, Caterpillar, El Gato:* to - geth - er we'll make ___ it right. __

Caterpillar, El Gato: When we get to - geth - er, it's tight. *Jack:* Yes! O - ver

riv - ers and val - leys, __ *El Gato:* o - ver moun - tains and streams, __ *Caterpillar:* o - ver

Jack, Caterpillar, El Gato: trag - ic fi - na - les, *Jack:* heart - bro - ken dreams, Ev - er true, ev - er dar - ing, *Jack:* ev - er for - ev - er swear - ing, *Jack, Caterpillar, El Gato:* we're gon - na make it, my friend. *Jack:* To - geth - er we're gon - na make it. *Rabbit:* I'm a - bout to get spayed. *Jack:* To - geth - er we're *Caterpillar, El Gato:* To - geth - er.

E♭maj9 B♭add2/D Cm7 Fsus4
gon - na make it. Rabbit: Did they sharp - en the blade? Jack: To - geth - er we're
To - geth - er.
E♭maj9 B♭add2/D Fadd2/A Gm7 Gm7/F
gon - na make it. Rabbit: But I won't be a - fraid. All: Gon - na
To - geth - er.
Cm7 B♭/D Cm7 Cm7/F
stand up to - geth - er. To - geth - er Jack: we'll get it right.
G♭/F A♭/F G♭/F A♭/F A B/A A

B/A
Em
D6
Cmaj13
A6/9
B5
C5
A♯5
B5
C5
A♯5
B5
C5
A♯5
B5
C5
E♭sus2
B♭/D
G♭sus2
D♭/F
E♭m
D♭/F
G♭sus2
E♭/F
F

G♭maj7
Fm7
G♭/A♭
E♭/F
Alice: 'Cause at the end of the day, we'll be to-geth-er a-gain.
Jack, Caterpillar, El Gato, Rabbit:
We'll be to - geth - er.
All: Un - til then…
E/F♯
To - geth - er we're
Emaj9
Badd2/D♯
gon - na make it through the
F♯add2/A♯
G♯m7
G♯m7/F♯
dark - est night. To - geth - er we're
Emaj9
Badd2/D♯
gon - na make it. Gon - na

C♯m7 F♯sus4 Emaj9 Badd2/D♯
make it back home. To - geth - er we're gon - na make it. Gon - na
F♯add2/A♯ G♯m7 G♯m7/F♯ C♯m7 B/D♯
stand up and fight 'cause to - geth - er is bet - ter. To -
E/F♯ F♯ G♯m/F♯ E/F♯ Emaj9 Badd2/D♯
geth - er Jack: we'll make it right.
Alice: We'll make it right.
(Gon - na make it through the

F♯add2/A♯ G♯m7 G♯m7/F♯ Emaj9 Badd2/D♯ C♯m7 F♯sus4
All: To - geth - er we're
dark - est night.
Gon - na make it, gon - na make it back home.
Emaj9 Badd2/D♯ F♯/A♯ G♯m7 G♯m7/F♯
gon - na make it
'cause to -
Gon - na make it. Stand up!)
C♯m7 B/D♯ E B/D♯
geth - er is bet - ter Alice: than what - ev - er I've done, yeah. All: To -

Chloe: geth-er is bet-ter than the pow-er of one.

All: To-geth-er's bet-ter *Jack:* than what-ev-er you might have planned.

Here I stand *All:* with

Al-ice in Won-der-land.

Heroes

Lyrics by
Jack Murphy

Music by
Frank Wildhorn

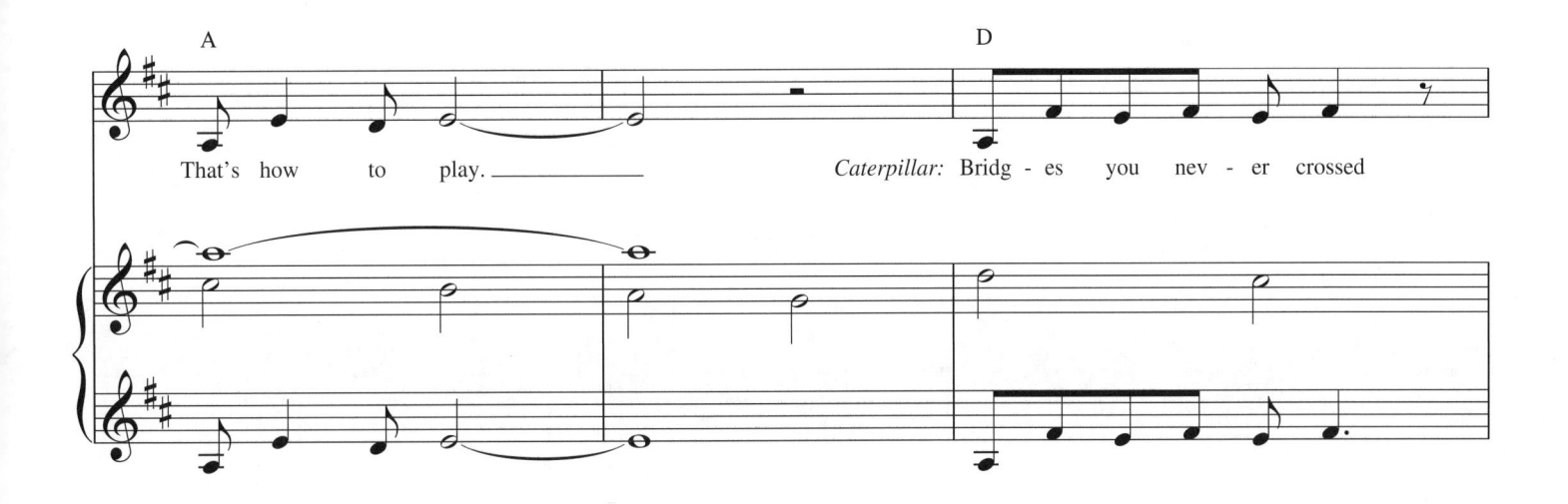

Moderately slow

Rabbit: Chances, they come and go, but you're afraid and so you run away.

El Gato: And when a chance is there, make believe you don't care.

That's how to play. *Caterpillar:* Bridges you never crossed

Copyright © 2011 Bronx Flash Music, Inc. (ASCAP), Ryan Samuel Melodies (ASCAP) and Lily Bird Music (BMI)
All Rights for the world Controlled and Administered by Bronx Flash Music, Inc. and Kenwon Music
International Copyright Secured   All Rights Reserved

left you a-lone and lost, look-ing a - round.

People are hard to find when they get left be-hind on such an - gry ground.

Moderately

Rabbit, El Gato, Caterpillar: So it goes... *Chloe:* The ho - urs move, the days go by.

We wait for he - roes to fall from the sky. Don't wait too long to learn what's true. I promise: you be a hero for me and I'll be a hero for you.

Alice: Nothing is black or white, easy as wrong or right, or so they say. You are the best of me saving the rest of me day after day.

Hold on to those you love through what you're dreaming of. You'll make it some-how.

The future can't change the past. Make ev-'ry sec-ond last,

for all we have is here and now.

All but Alice: The ho-urs move,

D/B D/A D/G D/F♯ Em7 G/A
the days go by. Why wait for he - roes to fall from the sky?
D D/C♯ D/B D/A D/G D/F♯
I fi - n'lly know what's real - ly true. I prom - ise:
Em7 Gsus2
you be a he - ro for me and I'll be a he - ro for you.
G D/A G/B A/C♯
Voice: I'll be a he - ro for you. All: I'll be a he - ro, a he -
Voice: I'll be a he - ro.
grad. cresc.

Em7
N.C.
G6/A
B♭
B♭/A
ro
for
you.
f
B♭/G
B♭/F
B♭/E♭
B♭/D
Cm7
E♭/F
B♭
B♭/A
B♭/G
B♭/F
B♭/E♭
B♭/D
All but Alice: The ho - urs move, the days go by. Why wait for
Cm7
E♭/F
B♭
B♭/A
B♭/G
B♭/F
he - roes to fall from the sky? The ho - urs move, the days go by.

B♭/E♭ B♭/D Cm7 E♭/F B♭ B♭/A
I'll be your he - ro. The hou - rs move,
mp
B♭/G B♭/F B♭/E♭ B♭/D Cm7 E♭/F
the days go by. Why wait for he - roes to fall?
B♭ B♭/A B♭/G B♭/F B♭/E♭ B♭/D
Chloe: The ho - urs move, the days go by. Why wait for
rit.
Cm7 E♭6/9 B♭
he - roes to fall from the sky?

Finding Wonderland

Lyrics by
Jack Murphy

Music by
Frank Wildhorn

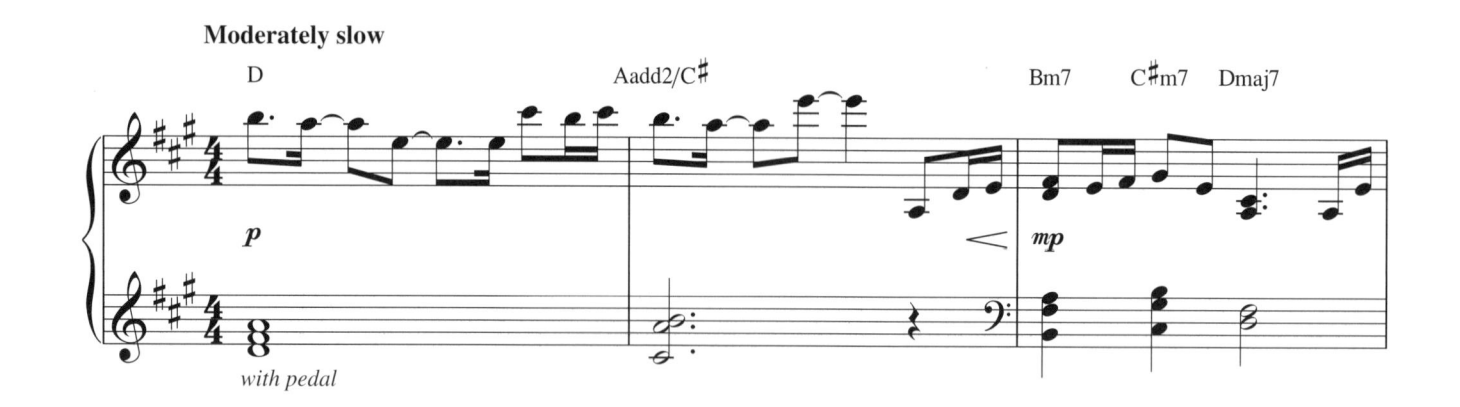

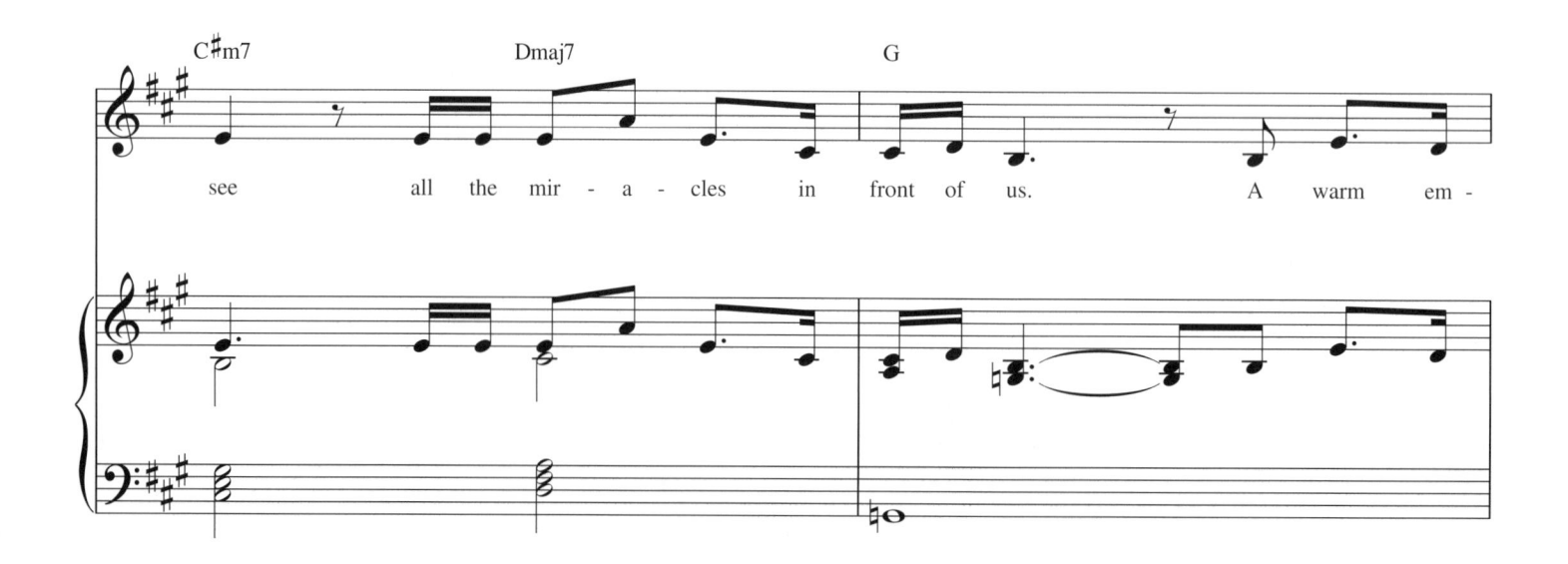

Moderately slow

Alice: We move too fast. We miss so much. We seldom see all the miracles in front of us. A warm em-

Copyright © 2011 Bronx Flash Music, Inc. (ASCAP), Ryan Samuel Melodies (ASCAP) and Lily Bird Music (BMI)
All Rights for the world Controlled and Administered by Bronx Flash Music, Inc. and Kenwon Music
International Copyright Secured   All Rights Reserved

brace, a hu-man touch... And so it goes. I race a-round, search high and low for the truth I used to know when there was mag-ic to be found. 'Cause finding Wonderland is taking time to see the child within who's always been there smiling back at me. So when I close my eyes, I just remember and I can't help finding Wonderland.

It's not too late, here in my prime. Hearts can un- break in the sto-ry's nick of time. A hap-py end-ing, a per-fect rhyme. 'Cause find-ing

Dadd2
Aadd2/C♯
Won - der - land is find - ing who you are: the child with - in
Bm7
D/E
G/A
A
who's al - ways been there like a shin - ing star. So when I
D
E/D
C♯m7
F♯m7
close my eyes, I see for - ev - er and I
Bm7
D/E
Asus4
A
keep on find - ing Won - der - land.

Ordinary magic happens ev'ry single day.
Wonderland is never far away. 'Cause finding
Wonderland is going home again to feel the love another gives and give it back. And then if you should

lose your way, reach out for some-one's hand, and you'll be find-ing Won-der-land.

You'll be find-ing Won-der-land.

More Great Piano/Vocal Books
FROM CHERRY LANE

For a complete listing of Cherry Lane titles available, including contents listings, please visit our web site at

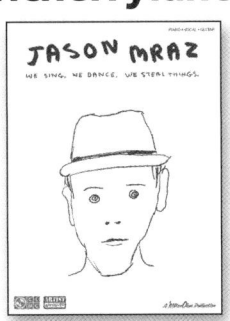

www.cherrylane.com

02501590	Sara Bareilles – Kaleidoscope Heart	$17.99
02501136	Sara Bareilles – Little Voice	$16.95
02501505	The Black Eyed Peas – The E.N.D.	$19.99
02502171	The Best of Boston	$17.95
02501123	Buffy the Vampire Slayer – Once More with Feeling	$18.95
02500665	Sammy Cahn Songbook	$24.95
02501454	Colbie Caillat – Breakthrough	$17.99
02501127	Colbie Caillat – Coco	$16.95
02500144	Mary Chapin Carpenter – Party Doll & Other Favorites	$16.95
02502165	John Denver Anthology – Revised	$22.95
02500002	John Denver Christmas	$14.95
02502166	John Denver's Greatest Hits	$17.95
02502151	John Denver – A Legacy in Song (Softcover)	$24.95
02502152	John Denver – A Legacy in Song (Hardcover)	$34.95
02500566	Poems, Prayers and Promises: The Art and Soul of John Denver	$19.95
02500326	John Denver – The Wildlife Concert	$17.95
02500501	John Denver and the Muppets: A Christmas Together	$9.95
02501186	The Dresden Dolls – The Virginia Companion	$39.95
02509922	The Songs of Bob Dylan	$29.95
02500497	Linda Eder – Gold	$14.95
02500396	Linda Eder – Christmas Stays the Same	$17.95
02500175	Linda Eder – It's No Secret Anymore	$14.95
02502209	Linda Eder – It's Time	$17.95
02500630	Donald Fagen – 5 of the Best	$7.95
02501542	Foreigner – The Collection	$19.99
02500535	Erroll Garner Anthology	$19.95
02500318	Gladiator	$12.95
02502126	Best of Guns N' Roses	$17.95
02502072	Guns N' Roses – Selections from Use Your Illusion I and II	$17.95
02500014	Sir Roland Hanna Collection	$19.95
02500856	Jack Johnson – Anthology	$19.95
02501140	Jack Johnson – Sleep Through the Static	$16.95
02501564	Jack Johnson – To the Sea	$19.99
02501546	Jack's Mannequin – *The Glass Passenger* and *The Dear Jack EP*	$19.99
02500381	Lenny Kravitz – Greatest Hits	$14.95
02501318	John Legend – Evolver	$19.99
02503701	Man of La Mancha	$11.95
02501047	Dave Matthews Band – Anthology	$24.95
02500693	Dave Matthews – Some Devil	$16.95
02502192	Dave Matthews Band – Under the Table and Dreaming	$17.95
02501514	John Mayer Anthology – Volume 1	$22.99
02501504	John Mayer – Battle Studies	$19.99
02500987	John Mayer – Continuum	$16.95
02500681	John Mayer – Heavier Things	$16.95
02500563	John Mayer – Room for Squares	$16.95
02500081	Natalie Merchant – Ophelia	$14.95
02500863	Jason Mraz – Mr. A-Z	$17.95
02501467	Jason Mraz – We Sing. We Dance. We Steal Things.	$19.99
02502895	Nine	$17.95
02501411	Nine – Film Selections	$19.99
02500425	Time and Love: The Art and Soul of Laura Nyro	$21.95
02502204	The Best of Metallica	$17.95
02501497	Ingrid Michaelson – Everybody	$17.99
02501496	Ingrid Michaelson – Girls and Boys	$19.99
02501529	Monte Montgomery Collection	$24.99
02501336	Amanda Palmer – Who Killed Amanda Palmer?	$17.99
02501004	Best of Gram Parsons	$16.95
02501137	Tom Paxton – Comedians & Angels	$16.95
02500010	Tom Paxton – The Honor of Your Company	$17.95
02507962	Peter, Paul & Mary – Holiday Concert	$17.95
02500145	Pokemon 2.B.A. Master	$12.95
02500026	The Prince of Egypt	$16.95
02500660	Best of Bonnie Raitt	$17.95
02502189	The Bonnie Raitt Collection	$22.95
02502088	Bonnie Raitt – Luck of the Draw	$14.95
02507958	Bonnie Raitt – Nick of Time	$14.95
02502218	Kenny Rogers – The Gift	$16.95
02501577	She & Him – Volume One	$16.99
02501578	She & Him – Volume Two	$17.99
02500414	Shrek	$16.99
02500536	Spirit – Stallion of the Cimarron	$16.95
02500166	Steely Dan – Anthology	$17.95
02500622	Steely Dan – Everything Must Go	$14.95
02500284	Steely Dan – Two Against Nature	$14.95
02500344	Billy Strayhorn: An American Master	$17.95
02500515	Barbra Streisand – Christmas Memories	$16.95
02507969	Barbra Streisand – A Collection: Greatest Hits and More	$17.95
02502164	Barbra Streisand – The Concert	$22.95
02500550	Essential Barbra Streisand	$24.95
02502228	Barbra Streisand – Higher Ground	$17.99
02501065	Barbra Streisand – Live in Concert 2006	$19.95
02501485	Barbra Streisand – Love Is the Answer	$19.99
02503617	John Tesh – Avalon	$15.95
02502178	The John Tesh Collection	$17.95
02503623	John Tesh – A Family Christmas	$15.95
02503630	John Tesh – Grand Passion	$16.95
02500307	John Tesh – Pure Movies 2	$16.95
02501068	The Evolution of Robin Thicke	$19.95
02500565	Thoroughly Modern Millie	$17.99
02501399	Best of Toto	$19.99
02502175	Tower of Power – Silver Anniversary	$17.95
02501403	Keith Urban – Defying Gravity	$17.99
02501008	Keith Urban – Love, Pain & The Whole Crazy Thing	$17.95
02501141	Keith Urban – Greatest Hits	$16.99
02502198	The "Weird Al" Yankovic Anthology	$17.95
02500334	Maury Yeston – December Songs	$17.95
02502225	The Maury Yeston Songbook	$19.95

See your local music dealer or contact:

cherry lane music company

EXCLUSIVELY DISTRIBUTED BY
HAL•LEONARD CORPORATION
7777 W. BLUEMOUND RD. P.O. BOX 13819 MILWAUKEE, WI 53213

Prices, contents and availability subject to change without notice.

0811

great songs series

This legendary series has delighted players and performers for generations.

Great Songs of Folk Music
Nearly 50 of the most popular folk songs of our time, including: Blowin' in the Wind • The House of the Rising Sun • Puff the Magic Dragon • This Land Is Your Land • Time in a Bottle • The Times They Are A-Changin' • The Unicorn • Where Have All the Flowers Gone? • and more.
02500997 P/V/G...$19.95

Great Songs from The Great American Songbook
52 American classics, including: Ain't That a Kick in the Head • As Time Goes By • Come Fly with Me • Georgia on My Mind • I Get a Kick Out of You • I've Got You Under My Skin • The Lady Is a Tramp • Love and Marriage • Mack the Knife • Misty • Over the Rainbow • People • Take the "A" Train • Thanks for the Memory • and more.
02500760 P/V/G...$16.95

Great Songs of the Movies
Nearly 60 of the best songs popularized in the movies, including: Accidentally in Love • Alfie • Almost Paradise • The Rainbow Connection • Somewhere in My Memory • Take My Breath Away (Love Theme) • Three Coins in the Fountain • (I've Had) the Time of My Life • Up Where We Belong • The Way We Were • and more.
02500967 P/V/G...$19.95

Great Songs of the Pop Era
Over 50 hits from the pop era, including: Every Breath You Take • I'm Every Woman • Just the Two of Us • Leaving on a Jet Plane • My Cherie Amour • Raindrops Keep Fallin' on My Head • Time After Time • (I've Had) the Time of My Life • What a Wonderful World • and more.
02500043 Easy Piano..$16.95

Great Songs for Weddings
A beautiful collection of 59 pop standards perfect for wedding ceremonies and receptions, including: Always and Forever • Amazed • Beautiful in My Eyes • Can You Feel the Love Tonight • Endless Love • Love of a Lifetime • Open Arms • Unforgettable • When I Fall in Love • The Wind Beneath My Wings • and more.
02501006 P/V/G...$19.95

Great Songs of the Fifties
Features rock, pop, country, Broadway and movie tunes, including: All Shook Up • At the Hop • Blue Suede Shoes • Dream Lover • Fly Me to the Moon • Kansas City • Love Me Tender • Misty • Peggy Sue • Rock Around the Clock • Sea of Love • Sixteen Tons • Take the "A" Train • Wonderful! Wonderful! • and more. Includes an introduction by award-winning journalist Bruce Pollock.
02500323 P/V/G...$16.95

Great Songs of the Sixties, Vol. 1 – Revised
The updated version of this classic book includes 80 faves from the 1960s: Angel of the Morning • Bridge over Troubled Water • Cabaret • Different Drum • Do You Believe in Magic • Eve of Destruction • Monday, Monday • Spinning Wheel • Walk on By • and more.
02509902 P/V/G...$19.95

Great Songs of the Sixties, Vol. 2 – Revised
61 more '60s hits: California Dreamin' • Crying • For Once in My Life • Honey • Little Green Apples • MacArthur Park • Me and Bobby McGee • Nowhere Man • Piece of My Heart • Sugar, Sugar • You Made Me So Very Happy • and more.
02509904 P/V/G...$19.95

Great Songs of the Seventies, Vol. 1 – Revised
This super collection of 70 big hits from the '70s includes: After the Love Has Gone • Afternoon Delight • Annie's Song • Band on the Run • Cold as Ice • FM • Imagine • It's Too Late • Layla • Let It Be • Maggie May • Piano Man • Shelter from the Storm • Superstar • Sweet Baby James • Time in a Bottle • The Way We Were • and more.
02509917 P/V/G...$19.95

Great Songs of the Nineties
Includes: Achy Breaky Heart • Beautiful in My Eyes • Believe • Black Hole Sun • Black Velvet • Blaze of Glory • Building a Mystery • Crash into Me • Fields of Gold • From a Distance • Glycerine • Here and Now • Hold My Hand • I'll Make Love to You • Ironic • Linger • My Heart Will Go On • Waterfalls • Wonderwall • and more.
02500040 P/V/G...$16.95

Great Songs of 2000-2009
Over 50 of the decade's biggest hits, including: Accidentally in Love • Breathe (2 AM) • Daughters • Hanging by a Moment • The Middle • The Remedy (I Won't Worry) • Smooth • A Thousand Miles • and more.
02500922 P/V/G...$24.99

Great Songs of Broadway – Revised Edition
This updated edition is loaded with 54 hits: And All That Jazz • Be Italian • Comedy Tonight • Consider Yourself • Dulcinea • Edelweiss • Friendship • Getting to Know You • Hopelessly Devoted to You • If I Loved You • The Impossible Dream • Mame • On My Own • On the Street Where You Live • People • Try to Remember • Unusual Way • When You're Good to Mama • Where Is Love? • and more.
02501545 P/V/G...$19.99

Great Songs for Children
90 wonderful, singable favorites kids love: Baa Baa Black Sheep • Bingo • The Candy Man • Do-Re-Mi • Eensy Weensy Spider • The Hokey Pokey • Linus and Lucy • Sing • This Old Man • Yellow Submarine • and more, with a touching foreword by Grammy-winning singer/songwriter Tom Chapin.
02501348 P/V/G...$19.99

Great Songs of Christmas
59 yuletide favorites in piano/vocal/guitar format, including: Breath of Heaven (Mary's Song) • Christmas Time Is Here • Frosty the Snow Man • I'll Be Home for Christmas • Jingle-Bell Rock • Nuttin' for Christmas • O Little Town of Bethlehem • Silver Bells • The Twelve Days of Christmas • What Child Is This? • and many more.
02501543 P/V/G...$17.99

Great Songs of Country Music
This volume features 58 country gems, including: Abilene • Afternoon Delight • Amazed • Annie's Song • Blue • Crazy • Elvira • Fly Away • For the Good Times • Friends in Low Places • The Gambler • Hey, Good Lookin' • I Hope You Dance • Thank God I'm a Country Boy • This Kiss • Your Cheatin' Heart • and more.
02500503 P/V/G...$19.95

cherry lane
music company

www.cherrylane.com

EXCLUSIVELY DISTRIBUTED BY
HAL•LEONARD CORPORATION
7777 W. BLUEMOUND RD. P.O. BOX 13819 MILWAUKEE, WI 53213

Prices, contents, and availability subject to change without notice.

0212